Theosis

Theosis

Patristic Remedy for Evangelical Yearning
at the Close of the Modern Age

Michael Paul Gama

Foreword by Gerald L. Sittser

WIPF & STOCK · Eugene, Oregon

THEOSIS
Patristic Remedy for Evangelical Yearning at the Close of the Modern Age

Wipf & Stock
An Imprint of Wipf and Stock Publishers
199 W. 8th Ave., Suite 3
Eugene, OR 97401

www.wipfandstock.com

PAPERBACK ISBN: 978-1-4982-9947-3
HARDCOVER ISBN: 978-1-4982-9949-7
EBOOK ISBN: 978-1-4982-9948-0

Manufactured in the U.S.A.   JANUARY 6, 2017

All biblical quotations are from the English Standard Version of the Bible, Crossway Bibles, 2003.

This book is dedicated to my parents, Margarita Delphina Noe Gama and Horacio Mario Gama, now having taken their places among that great cloud of witnesses. To my mother, who never wearied in her quest to experience more of Jesus and his life. And to my father, whose calm and quiet articulation of his own faith I initially misunderstood as reticence. It was only later, in my maturity, that I understood it for what it was—a vision laden with awe and wonder. Thank you. Please pray for us.

"He became human that we might become divine."

St. Athanasius

"Did you hear what he said? Us lions. That means him and me. Us lions. That's what I like about Aslan. No side. No stand-off-ishess. Us lions. That meant him and me."

C.S. Lewis, *The Lion, the Witch and the Wardrobe*

Contents

Foreword

I grew up in the 50s and 60s. I witnessed both the peak and decline of Christendom in America. The fears and opportunities of this brief postwar period epitomized the heyday of mainline Protestant Christianity. We still prayed in public schools and pledged allegiance to the flag of a nation that thought of itself as living "under God." Protestant leaders could still make pronouncements that presidents listened and responded to. Their opinions mattered that much. Of course we know now that all was not well. But it really doesn't matter much anyway. For we are quickly leaving behind that idyllic age (or so it seemed at the time). We have now entered a new religious phase of American history. It is probably for the best that we have.

The signs are apparent everywhere. The Christian movement is growing in the Global South but declining in Europe and North America. Europe is now post-Christian, and the United States is clearly moving in the same direction. The presence of megachurches notwithstanding, much of Christianity in the West seems old and tired, gasping for breath.

I see it in my students. I teach in a Christian liberal arts university on the West Coast. I keep track of many students after they graduate. They face a lot of turbulence. Some drift from church and faith altogether. They leave the faith not because argument persuades them but because secularity absorbs them. They are breathing a different air. It is the air of relativism and tolerance and pluralism, the air of postmodernity.

They live in a different world from the one in which I grew up. My seminary education was pure Reformation and evangelical Christianity—Luther and Calvin, Wesley and Whitfield, evangelism and preaching and small groups. My students are less persuaded by the family arguments of the Reformation. When they hear that Luther walked out on a meeting with Zwingli over a disagreement concerning the meaning of four words ("This is my body"), they sigh in disbelief. They are less moved by the method of evangelical conversion too. When they learn about the eighteenth-century evangelical awakening, they relish the stories but raise questions about the superficiality. They respond more positively to Wesley's method of disciple-making than they do to his method of mass evangelism.

But these same students cannot get enough of the early Christian period. The stories and theology and practices captivate them. They rediscover Trinitarian faith as a vital belief system that has practical consequences for how faith actually functions. They study the catechumenate with genuine curiosity, asking how it can be revived today. They fall in love with the Desert Fathers and Mothers, wondering what being a "spiritual athlete" would require today. They applaud how the early Christian movement grew so steadily over such a long period of time before it received any form of state support. The faith of the church back then seems more vital to them, more whole and healthy—flesh, blood, and bones, not just skin. They join a growing chorus of voices that cries, "Back to the future!"

Enter Michael Gama. Michael has written a marvelous and ambitious book—part historical narrative, part theological tract, part apologia, part pastoral letter, part prophetic call. He is summoning the church to travel "back to the future." There is a thread of autobiography in the book. He tells his own story to illustrate why the subject matters to him and why it should matter to us. I found his story useful and compelling, though never intrusive and excessive. Just enough, but not too much. He also explains how we arrived where we are today—how the Middle Ages gave way to the Renaissance, how the Renaissance gave way to the Enlightenment and modern evangelicalism, how both Enlightenment and evangelicalism have given way to postmodernism. He reintroduces the beauty and complexity and cogency of early Christianity, which to Michael culminated in the doctrine—the reality—of *theosis*. This is more than rational faith, though not less. This is mystical union with God and utter transformation of the whole of life.

Michael is an intellectual. But he is also a prophet and a pastor, which makes this book not only informative but also winsome, compelling, and accessible. He writes as believer and advocate. A child of the same world in which we all live, he has rediscovered ancient Christianity and sees it not as a dead tradition but as a living faith that is calling us back to something old that can become new again. He is commanding the bones to come back to life. In his mind they were never dead.

I have never personally met Michael. But we have corresponded a great deal. I like his heart as well as his mind, his convictions as well as his ideas. I commend this book to you, the reader. He invites us to join him on a journey—or more appropriately, a pilgrimage—to explore what has been lost to the memory of the church but can be found again. He is a trustworthy guide who will help us do the finding. I am one who is ready to follow.

Gerald L. Sittser
Professor of Theology, Whitworth University

Acknowledgments

For a book whose development and writing spans several years, a complete list of those for whose help and encouragement I am so grateful would be unwieldy. There are, however, a number I would so like to specifically thank, beginning with numerous excellent teachers, including Brendan Furnish, Tom Soule, Don Haas, Daniel Tappeiner, and Daniel Brunner.

I am also indebted to close friends for their continued encouragement as I sought to make sense of my own spiritual pilgrimage and its place within the overall ecclesiological context of our times, particularly David Snell and Jeff Andrus.

Also, I am especially grateful to my Abouna, Jonathan Dekker, and the Maronite Monks of Jesus, Mary, and Joseph, who gave me their blessing and encouragement for this project.

Finally, and most significantly, without the loving support and continued encouragement of my wife, Carol, and our three children, Jordan, Jessica, and David, none of this would have ever happened. Thank you so much.

Introduction

The study that follows is, in part, a personal story—a story that touches on my spiritual pilgrimage from Roman Catholicism, through evangelicalism, and back to Maronite Catholicism, one of the several ancient Eastern Catholic churches in full fellowship with Rome.

But this sharing of portions of my own story would likely be of marginal interest except insofar, as I have come to suspect, that it may parallel and perhaps even anticipate the greater story of challenge and change that is rapidly overtaking today's American evangelicalism.

When, many years ago, I concluded that, insofar as I understood it, evangelicalism and its churches was no longer "working for me," I was a statistical outlier. I made my exit quietly, unnoticed, and alone. In the main, it seemed at that time that for most evangelicals all was still (very) well. I left the fold, fatigued by what I perceived as evangelicalism's frenzied efforts to continually generate an exciting "next new thing." I had grown tired of programs, weary of campaigns, and bored and put off by increasingly sophisticated and dazzling Sunday performances that seemed to increase in their vacuousness even as their production values soared to approach near theatrical-level quality.

But even more pressing than my tiring of the packaging and presentation of the evangelicalism I experienced at the close of the twentieth century was my suspicion—my hope—that there had to be more to the faith than I enjoyed or could see evidenced around me in the churches we attended. And while there was no shortage of exciting programs, and seemingly no end to outreaches and ministries, I searched in vain for what I hoped must be the substance of our historic faith—that substance evidenced in the lives of the patriarchs who walked with God, talked with God, and knew him as a friend knows a friend.

Of course, the argument could be made that I alone was "missing it," and that I alone was a dissatisfied malcontent, grousing alone while surrounded by fellow believers living exciting and full lives of spiritual victory and purpose. And, were that the case, then my personal spiritual pilgrimage might simply be the familiar story of one struggling back to the church and formation of his youth.

On the other hand, while my own withdrawal from evangelicalism represented not even a trickle toward the exits, the current tsunami of younger evangelicals who are fleeing the churches of their childhood is remarkable. And troubling. Even secular demographers have noted that while the percentages of youths now self-identifying as evangelical have drastically diminished over the past decade or two, the ranks of those now claiming "none," as in "none of the above," for their religious or church affiliation have swelled. Clearly, in today's evangelical world, nothing is not happening. It is in light of this exodus that my own story perhaps has relevance. And while it can be hazardous and unproductive to generalize, I believe I have detected in my own experience hints as to the reasons behind the current evacuation of youth from evangelicalism today.

Of course, it is likely that there are as many reasons for this current exodus as there are individuals making their escape. Even so, the magnitude of the departure hints at significant underlying cultural shifts so sweeping and so fundamental as to suggest that we are in the throes of a dramatic, overarching paradigm shift—a process described years ago by the physicist Thomas Kuhn. If so, perhaps we might rightly wonder if classical evangelicalism now finds itself in the challenging position of speaking most articulately to the concerns of a fading paradigm. If this is at all true, then it might help explain why evangelicalism now seems to speak less authoritatively and persuasively to a growing number of youthful believers who are experiencing their formation in a new epoch.

Perhaps it is helpful to consider a thought experiment. Let us, for argument's sake, imagine classical evangelicalism as a cultural "product" which thrived for as long as it provided adequate and satisfying answers for people beset by the questions related to living in the modern world. Evangelicalism was then widely "consumed" because it widely "satisfied." But what happens when evangelicalism is asked different questions? And what happens when these different questions are being asked by a new and younger generation, many of whom are reporting that they are no longer receiving answers that satisfy, or make sense, or fulfill their spiritual longing?

INTRODUCTION

What I wish to show in the pages that follow is that a growing number of—especially younger—Americans no longer see the world through the rationalistic, either/or lens of twentieth-century modernity. And because of this, while their father's evangelicalism might have been the answer to the pressing questions of his day, many of the questions themselves have seemingly shifted, and many of the traditional (evangelical) answers and positions no longer seem adequate. Put another way, is it possible that classical evangelicalism is, at least in part, the answer to questions that a declining number of people are even asking?

My thesis is that the answer to this important question could be "yes," and I seek to show the development of this growing disconnect. I seek as well to chronicle how, at its roots, evangelicalism is the sibling of the Enlightenment, and that together they share and embrace the same rationalistic presuppositions that underlie twentieth-century modernity. Likewise, I will attempt to explain how, for many years, this sibling relationship was amicable and even co-enabling . . . until it wasn't.

I will also recount how, while few perhaps even noticed, the philosophical and cultural paradigm of ebbing twentieth-century modernity was developing a serious case of dry rot in those dusk years. This systemic weakening wasn't apparent at first, and even when it became so it was disregarded by many as unimportant, or simply silly, and of no consequence. Nonetheless, when a tipping point was reached, the shifting of paradigms was radical, quick, and catholic. The emperor, indeed, acquired a new mind, and with it a radically altered understanding of the world, and of reality.

Evangelicalism, lacking any magisterium or central, unified guiding counsel, has responded to the advent of this new mind-consciousness, or paradigm, in predictably diverse fashion. While some seem resolute in its rejection, others embrace it and proclaim, under its influence, that insofar as evangelicalism is concerned, "everything must change!"

I personally discern more wisdom in those voices who embrace neither extreme, but are rather counseling for a revisiting of central evangelical themes, particularly soteriology. It is precisely this revisiting of the salvific mystery that I propose presents the greatest opportunity for evangelicals as they seek to move productively into the twenty-first century.

It seems evident that the tight rationalistic parameters of an ebbing modernity are increasingly losing their hegemony over the minds and hearts of a younger generation of evangelicals busily constructing their own understanding of reality. And as this is happening, decidedly nonmodern and arguably even premodern values, such as mystery, wonder, and an openness to previously rejected traditions and customs, are being considered.

In this spirit, I am suggesting that the road forward for evangelicalism lies in a radical reexamination of the fundamentals of our faith—one certainly embracing mystery, wonder, and an openness to the ancient Christian understanding of salvation itself.

I propose in the pages that follow that the ancient (Eastern) Christian doctrine of salvation—*theosis*, or union with God (divinization)—can provide a road map for an evangelicalism caught between two ages, searching for a fruitful road ahead as it negotiates its way from modernity into postmodernity.

The doctrine and promise of *theosis*—that God became human so that humanity may become God—not by nature, but by grace—is, as I will attempt to show, central to the faith of a critical mass of Christians worldwide. Likewise, as the patristic understanding, it is neither new nor innovative. It is, instead, one is tempted to say, "mere Christianity."

If the promise of so great a salvation can indeed be understood as true, traditional, and central to our faith, then everything has certainly changed. As such, and with this new (actually, ancient) understanding, salvation can no longer be understood as an exclusively personal and individual phenomenon, but, instead, can now be gazed at through a patristic lens viewing redemption as a joyous and wondrous event that leaves no corner of the cosmos untouched.

Finally, I have attempted to write the book I would have wanted to have available when my own journey from evangelicalism began—a book that perhaps, even in a small way, speaks to the yearning for "more" that so many post-evangelical millennials now voice.

Nonetheless, a caution is in order. In the spirit of the Eastern fathers, staretzy, and desert saints, I have done my best to write nothing new, nor explore or suggest any theological or spiritual innovations. Instead, I have simply sought to reintroduce an understanding of our great and mysterious faith that has been embraced for so long in the Christian East, though hidden for a time from much of the Christian West. In this, mine is simply one voice of a growing number, excited, as were King Josiah's men, when they rediscovered "the Book of the Law in the temple of the LORD."

May God be with us as we seek to rediscover and live our ancient/future faith and become "new men and women," partaking of the divine nature and filled with all the fullness of God.

Pentecost 2016

1

Genesis

"I give praise to your holy Nature, Lord, for you have made my nature a sanctuary for your hiddenness and a tabernacle for your holy mysteries, a place where you can dwell and a holy temple for your Divinity."[1]

—St. Isaac the Syrian

I WAS BORN AND baptized Roman Catholic. This in itself isn't necessarily remarkable, particularly since both my parents were first-generation Americans, born of parents newly arrived from Mexico. They had migrated northward, bereft of nearly everything save hope. At that time, being Mexican meant being Catholic. And so, Catholic we were.

I remember as a young child visiting my mother's mother, my little *abuelita*, in her tiny, dark Los Angeles duplex. These visits were fine until I invariably had to use the bathroom. I dreaded this, as there was only one way to get there—through her bedroom. Her bedroom seemed permanently dark, even in midday, smelling slightly medicinal. Even in my child's mind I could understand *medicinal*. After all, my grandmother was by this time quite elderly—in retrospect, at least fifty-five!

Quickly traversing her bedroom, I could never negotiate the entire transit without stealing a furtive glance at the large framed picture of the Sacred Heart of Jesus hanging above her bureau. I remember liking Jesus, even at that young age, but I didn't find this image particularly consoling.

1. Fr. Stephen, "Words," lines 104–6.

In fact it was, in a word, terrifying. The darkness didn't help, and neither did the candles, burning silently beneath the large framed image. Walking quickly beneath it, past the candles and her prayer beads sitting atop the chest of drawers, I was left with just one remaining challenge. I still had to make it past the large, foreboding crucifix of Our Lord, hanging in still, silent agony on the adjacent wall. The bathroom visit completed, I would retreat back through the bedroom in a near run, exhilarated by my successful transit and escape. Not wishing to betray my fears, I would slow to a walk, exiting the bedroom into the narrow kitchen, coolly and casually.

These visits to my grandmother's house were, of course, complemented by church attendance itself. I remember St. Catherine's as a cool, yawning, and cavernous edifice, internally adorned with statues, icons, an elaborate prayer rail, high ceilings and a mass uttered in a foreign tongue. This was pre-Vatican II Roman Catholicism, in all its austerity and *mysterium tremendum*, degrees of which would be stripped away in the upcoming worldwide Church Council.

At my young age, I would not yet have known how to articulate this sense of *mysterium tremendum* I felt as I walked into that church—or even into my grandmother's bedroom. I felt an awe, and even a bit of fear, in both contexts but wasn't sure exactly why.

But the Catholicism of my birth was left behind when my mother met a kind, evangelical Black man sharing the "Plan of Salvation" door-to-door, reading to her from his Bible. Being ethnically Catholic, especially in the pre-Vatican II Church, my mother had never actually read the Bible herself, this being a task best left to the priests. But for my mother, spiritually serious and intent, reading the Scriptures awakened her from her spiritual slumber. She got saved! And in her gratitude and enthusiasm we were thus blasted out of the Catholic Church forever. Or so it seemed.

Our next years were spent as itinerate evangelicals, moving through a series of church experiences. These experiences ranged from small churches to even smaller ones, as my parents searched for a pastor and community with which they felt comfortable, and which they perceived as sufficiently serious and intentional about the faith. I most enjoyed our little Covenant Church in Hawthorne, California, where my aunt, uncle, and cousins—new evangelicals themselves—also attended. They lived near the church and we would often be there after services, for lunch and lounging. I made friends with the neighbor boy and with the Wilson brothers at the end of the block. We played football in the street until the brothers' musical interests overshadowed their athletic interests and they left the streets for the recording studio and became the Beach Boys. Their exodus broke up our street football teams.

After we left the Covenant Church, we continued our migration through a series of even smaller churches. For my parents, programs, glitz, and pastoral charisma would not suffice. What they required was a pastor who "knew God," and such pastors were typically not the celebrated leaders of the "fastest growing church in . . . [fill in the name of the city, county, or even state here]."

Early in our evangelical experience, though still a young child, I would often speak with my mother about our newfound faith. In one of our talks, she passionately expressed her desire to pursue and know God, vowing, "If all being saved meant was that you lived your life and then died and went to heaven, I'd say, 'To hell with it,' and just live my life." As a child, hearing this was startling and a bit upsetting. It took me a few days of mulling this over until I concluded that my mother was not simply being blasphemously flippant, but instead was passionately expressing her burning, near-desperate desire to experience God in a real, personal, and life-changing way. When I finally understood this, I agreed with her.

Being in the evangelical world meant that my adolescence was filled with youth groups, missions trips, and engagements with groups like Youth for Christ and Young Life. I was never a joiner, and at times found the get-togethers and games that so often defined these groups challenging. Even so, I was grateful for the organizers and their diligent and selfless work on our behalf, and remain so today.

Though my parents themselves had never attended college, it was assumed that I would. So when the time came to select a school, my choices narrowed to two options. One was a fine evangelical school in the Midwest, offset by its perfectly acceptable West Coast complement. Budding pedagogue that I wasn't, and more interested in running cross-country than academics, I opted for the Western choice with its rolling hills and national championship cross-country program. I couldn't imagine running in snow.

When the time came for me to begin cross-country camp that late August prior to my first freshman semester, my family drove me up the highway to the beautiful seaside school. Our valiant though aging '56 Chevy station wagon, acrid smoke billowing from beneath the dashboard, coughed and lurched its way up the final mile leading to the school's entrance. I had arrived. I was thus deposited into the care of one of evangelicalism's two most iconic symbols of Christian higher education. I was excited. My father gravely shook my hand; my mother wept at the prospect of her first-born leaving home. Her tears surprised me and I recall vaguely wondering what her problem could be.

I liked school, though it did present a significant cultural shock. The monochromatic demographic and uni-cultural ethnic flavor was different, and I discovered that many of the assumptions I had held as self-evident cultural truths weren't necessarily universal. Worse, I had never eaten food like that before. There wasn't a tortilla or jalapeño in sight. Fortunately, one cross-country teammate was also Hispanic. We glommed onto each other like long-lost brothers and, whenever our flimsy budgets could manage, escaped down the hill and fled into the city over to the wrong side of the tracks for some "real" food. Overall, college was an acceptable four years.

Though ensconced directly in the belly of the evangelical beast, I had a spotty church experience during my college years. I tried. I visited a number of churches, especially early on, finally giving up. Nothing worked. Perhaps it was the transitory nature of college life that made satisfaction with a church impossible. Compounding the problem, I couldn't shake the remembrance of my mother's passionate vow of many years before. I didn't know what, exactly, I was looking for, but knew enough to know that what I had experienced to that point fell short. Way short. I wanted something *real*. I yearned for something of my faith beyond what I had experienced and beyond whatever it was that I saw around me. Surely, I thought, there *had* to be more to the faith than *this*.

Though driven by spiritual desire, not knowing where to look compounded my frustration. I read widely, in what I supposed were ancient and mystical Christian writings. I was fascinated that there seemed to be people who truly encountered God, and that God seemed to actually reveal himself to them. He spoke, and they listened. It seemed they could actually hear and truly experience him. As for me, I was simply frustrated, essentially capable of neither. In my desperation, I cast my nets widely, reading and experimenting with a wild lack of discipline bred of ignorance. Finally, one afternoon, hunched over the *Tibetan Book of the Dead*, searching for something—anything—I concluded that my spiritual quest and yearning had perhaps led me a bit too far afield. I retreated back in the direction of what I assumed was Christian orthodoxy.

Pivoting in my reading to focus more on the mystics of the Western church, I hopscotched around, growing ever more convinced that there was a legitimate legacy of people who had truly encountered God, acutely aware that I was far from understanding their experiences, and even farther from experiencing anything like this myself. Despite my frustration, it was becoming increasingly more obvious that there *was* more to this faith than I had been taught or exposed to, and far more even than I had ever imagined. Though they spoke with different voices, articulating differing experiences, the mystics' stories seemed to generally yield one basic conclusion. They had, in some sense and in some manner, "seen God." Of course, they never claimed to have visually encountered him in a concrete sense, but the "union" with God of which they wrote left me mystified, though exhilarated. Perhaps, whatever they had experienced was related to the *more* of the faith I desperately yearned for and hoped was there. And unless these mystics were all delusional, this *more* seemed to have something to do with being united with God, or "unioned" with him. Whatever that meant, I wasn't much sure. Nonetheless, this was the point at which I had arrived in my reading and thinking when I stepped into the fellowship hall on a mild spring evening in the upscale evangelical church just down the hill from the college.

Union with God—Encountered and Communicated—Poorly

Along with several friends, I had signed on to spend the summer in the High Sierras as a counselor, working with inner-city kids in a rigorous outdoor program. The leader of the program had managed to bring in a highly recognized evangelical leader to keynote our first meeting together. He was to inspire and perhaps even dazzle us with the opportunities our coming summer of service would hold.

I guess I hadn't really been listening when he came to a pause in his presentation and asked for questions or comments. I suppose, too, he was working hard to corral a group of energized college students, and saying whatever he could to motivate us for the coming summer. In contrast, I was thinking about mystics and union and dreaming about how this all might work. Or *could* work, that is, if it was at all truly real. I hoped it was. I was desperate for it to be so. It *had* to be real. I was busy mulling over the ramifications of all of this when, somewhere off in the distance, I heard the speaker ask for comments. There was a pause, and then a silence. No one spoke. So I did because it had just dawned on me how it was all supposed to work, how it was all supposed to fit, and the ramifications of it all. Or so I thought.

"Yes, uh . . . I do have a comment." I continued, tentatively, picking up steam.

"I get it now," I offered. "I get it. *I'm* Jesus Christ. Or am supposed to be." I sat back in awe of what I had just come to and just uttered. Others sat, as well, though hardly in awe. Twenty nervous collegians shifted in their seats as I waited for them to recognize the gravity and magnificence of what I had just offered.

What's a speaker to do with *that*? Even a well-known, polished, and admired evangelical icon? I suppose he did just about what anyone else would in that situation, especially, as in fairness to him, he hadn't been privy to the conversation that had taken place in my head and heart over the past minutes, and months.

"Well, you sure don't look like Jesus to *me*," he blurted, with no small measure of triumph. Past the superficial, I had to admit, he had a point. Bearded and with shoulder-length hair, I may indeed have looked *something* like Jesus may have looked. But beyond that, the speaker was absolutely correct. I bore little resemblance to my Lord in any significant way. And I knew it.

At his glib riposte, the silent students erupted in nervous laughter. The leader, now firmly back in control, pursued his prepared talk for a few more minutes, and then dismissed us into the mild Santa Barbara evening for a timely break.

"What the heck? What were you *thinking*?" My scraggly-bearded friend moved alongside me as we slowly walked into the church garden. "I'm Jesus Christ. *Huh?*"

"Bob," I chuckled, "don't you get it? Of course I am. Or at least I'm *supposed* to be. And so are you. That's the whole thing to all this. All this stuff about 'Christ in us,' and us being 'filled with all the fullness of God'—that doesn't mean nothing. It can't, and in fact it means *everything*. Or should." We walked along in silence.

"Besides," I continued, "what about the mystics? They seemed to encounter God in amazing ways and wound up writing about it and talking as thought they were actually, *really*, united with him, to the point at which it seemed they loved him, lived in him, and were maybe even one with him in some sense. I mean, at least close enough to where it didn't seem like there was much distance between them. Not like we live. Or at least, not like I live."

"I don't know. Maybe you're right," Bob mused. "But you can't just run around in churches proclaiming, 'I'm Jesus Christ.'" I had to admit, he did have a point.

"I suppose you're right," I surrendered. "But, doggone, there's gotta be more to all this than just *this*," I asserted in final protest. "You don't really think this is all there is to this, do you?" I asked, waving my arm in a large arc to take in the church and its beautiful grounds.

Hopes for Union Collide with Ministry Opportunities

I heeded my friend's advice, and over the next years carefully avoided any and all public outbursts proclaiming even vague similitude to our Lord. I ultimately graduated from that evangelical college, and went on to graduate from a well-regarded evangelical seminary. And yet, by the time I reached the midpoint of my seminary experience, I knew I could never be a pulpit pastor, or pastor any evangelical church. Perhaps I was damaged goods, but my faith didn't seem to be working for me any more with an MDiv than it had in the years before I had even finished college. As a system, evangelical-ism seemed to me to be broken. I didn't want to pastor the "fastest growing church" of anywhere. I didn't want to pound the drum and run programs. I didn't want to be responsible for getting people enthused or excited. I couldn't even manage to get myself enthused. And I certainly didn't want to start out, like a number of my friends had, cutting my pastoral teeth on a junior high school group. I would be miserable and they would be worse. We'd hate each other for sure, and under my brilliant leadership I was con-fident any such group would grind down to about three miserable souls. I couldn't bear the thought of making a living doing something within a system I couldn't absolutely believe in. I didn't feel it would be honest.

Even so, with a young family, I couldn't do nothing. So I went into advertising. I spent my days and years strategizing how to get people to buy stuff. I figured they didn't have to buy anything if they didn't want to. They had a choice. Most of the products our clients were selling weren't life-or-death issues. Sometimes prospects bought; usually they didn't. An honest business. I made a living—at times a good one. And though, over the years, I have encountered a sprinkling of people whose business mo-tives may have been less than laudable, in the main, I have been privileged and humbled to work alongside many honorable and talented colleagues. I learned a lot. It has been fun.

But through these years, the nagging, yearning urge for something *more* never left. I continued to read the mystics and of the wonder of their lives. I contemplated the idea of union with God and the possibilities it might hold. I concluded, among other things, that prayer was central and that I knew nothing of it. Not really. I launched into an experiment with prayer that, while pitiful in its naiveté and simplicity, nonetheless must have somehow attracted the grace and mercy of God. My prayers ultimately yielded a life-changing silence and presence I had never before imagined possible. God was gracious.

Meanwhile, still in evangelicalism, my frustration and dissatisfaction continued to mount. It seemed so crimped, so hard-edged, so hemmed in, and so set on needing to package and market the Next Big Thing. Where was the wonder? The mystery? I hated the programs. I didn't want to be excited or enthused. Or worked. Heck, I was in advertising and marketing five, sometimes six days a week. I didn't want it on the seventh. And especially not from a pastor freshly returned from a conference on how to use marketing skills to grow his church. There *had* to be more.

When the break finally came, it wasn't so much a beckoning out of evangelicalism as much as it was a shove out the door. I didn't do or say anything wrong, but merely asked questions and was reminded firsthand that (as we used to caution each other in business), "the torso must survive." In this particular instance, I certainly wasn't the torso. Not even close. I was expendable. Though our experience in and expulsion from this particular small church was disappointing, I am thankful now, for the opportunity I was given to stop, reset, and rethink important issues related to the nature of the church and faith itself.

The Break with Evangelicalism
and Rediscovery of an Ancient Past

Once the break with our small evangelical church was accomplished, the stage was set for the move away from Evangelicalism itself. Once freed from the narrow parameters of this particular community, I began to wriggle free from the slightly larger confines of overall evangelicalism. This process was driven by revisiting questions I had simply assumed were already answered. Questions like, "What is church, or *the church*?" were joined by others such as, "What, *really*, is Communion, or the Eucharist?" I wondered, as well, "What do the (so-called) fathers have to say about these and other issues? And should it even matter?" I considered too, "What of that large percentage of non-Western Christendom that believes and worships differently than we do, and has for nearly two thousand years? What, if anything, does their faith mean to and for me?"

While I was the beneficiary of an adequate college education, along with solid seminary schooling, I realized my exposure to the fathers and mothers of the ancient church—East and West—was scant. Seeking to correct this deficiency, I spent the next years in a focused study of their history, lives, and works. I added to this the writings of the desert dwellers, hermits, monks, and mystics, and my vision of our faith was vastly broadened and deepened.

Even after numerous years of focused study, I certainly did not become an expert in these ancient writings or spiritualties. But of several things I became very convinced. First, I grew to understand that the church did not begin with Aimee Semple McPherson. Or even Luther and the Reformers. I also learned that the church and our faith are not, either in their origin or theologies, exclusively and ultimately Western, and as such have no enduring obligation to live and express truth within the confines or parameters of Western rationality or sensibilities. In fact, I concluded that, in a very significant sense, our faith is an *Eastern* religion. Finally, I also concluded that the articulation of our evangelical faith within the paradigm of, and with the terminologies most hospitable to, the Western, rationalistic Enlightenment tradition might at some point come to be regarded as a historic anomaly.

Millennials and the Radical Changes They Bring to Evangelicalism

I am not a millennial. Far from it. But as a post-evangelical surveying the contemporary evangelical scene, I cannot help but note in the current mass exodus of evangelical millennials from their churches parallels to my own story. Of course, in every generation, youths' reasons for abandoning the churches and even the faith of their parents range from the significant to the silly to the merely self-serving. That's expected. Even so, when a critical mass of thoughtful millennials gives voice to a yearning for an authentic encounter with God, protesting that the current ecclesial situation no longer "works" for them, serious (and older) evangelicals should take note. I suspect, too, that attempts to simply repackage and represent a tired product will be quickly sniffed out and rejected by discerning youths. Again, evangelical elders should take note.

My own desire to understand the contemporary situation is the catalyst for the study that follows. In the sections below, I seek that understanding by first exploring the origins of evangelicalism and particularly its relationship to the Enlightenment. This is followed by a survey of our contemporary culture and its relationship to the formation of evangelicals, especially the youth.

If this study concluded at that point, it would certainly be on a downbeat. Instead, I see much to be hopeful for, and conclude on a hopeful note. True, if one is wedded to the "way things have always been," disappointment likely awaits. It is just as true, however, that change for the sake of change is foolhardy. Instead, I see, and seek to present, a reason for hope, particularly as I see a growing number of serious evangelicals exploring their common heritage in the ancient, historical church. Likewise, I argue for a revisiting of the ancient Christian soteriological understanding and suggest that an Enlightenment-formed evangelicalism has truncated and even defanged the evangelical model of salvation. I believe that it is this truncating and defanging that many millennials reflexively reject. I am encouraged to note that this proposal is reflected in the thinking and writing of a growing number of influential evangelical thinkers and theologians.

A crucial part of this reexamination of the means and meaning of historic, orthodox Christian soteriology will entail a rediscovery and recognition that wonder and mystery lie at the heart of our ancient/present faith. It will also entail recognition that, at its core, His story—*our* story—is a *love* story of redemption and restoration. As the Greek Orthodox Bishop Maximos Aghiorgoussis suggests, our salvation story can be no less than the "restoration of life in communion with God."[2] Indeed, a story truly worthy of God himself can be nothing less, and if true, then all *has* changed.

As the ancients taught, to aspire to full humanity is to aspire to life in full communion with God. The stakes are high, and humanity alone will not be the sole winners in this great exchange of his divinity for our humanity. Echoing St. Maximus the Confessor, Aghiorgoussis also suggests that all creation awaits our response to the divine *Eros* or reaching out to humankind, and that related to our response will be the bringing

2. Meyendorff and Tobias, *Salvation*, 36.

of all "creation into communion with God."[3] This, indeed, is our intended destiny—*theosis*, or communion (union) with God. But the fullness of this vision, suggests evangelical theologian Scot McKnight, can only be realized if we exchange our traditional evangelical concept of our salvation—the wondrous, though still truncated, Plan of Salvation—for the robust and full-bodied *gospel of Jesus Christ*. In the pages that follow I seek to show how and why this exchange is needed, and how it is ultimately grounded in the "Exchange Formula"[4] written of and understood by the ancients as mere Christianity.

3. Ibid., 37.

4. Norman Russell explains, regarding the Eastern Christian understanding of *theosis*, that, "It has the structural significance that determines our whole understanding of salvation and the conduct which ought to flow from it. The Fathers expressed this in what has come to be known as the 'Exchange Formula.'" (*Fellow Workers with God*, [AQ page]).

2

Philosophical Origins and the Evolution
From the Premodern to the Modern

> *"The safest general characterization of the philosophical tradition is that it consists of a series of footnotes to Plato."*[1]
>
> —Alfred North Whitehead

I AM MY FATHER'S son. But, sadly, I did not inherit his brain. So any facility he had—and it was formidable—for numbers and math leapt over me, with the greatest of ease, to the following generation. Nonetheless, even at a young age I was fascinated by the *idea* behind math. That is to say, if 2 + 2 = 4, I wondered, did it equal 4 because that was the way the universe was constructed, or did 2 + 2 equal 4 because humans had simply decided it did? Off and on, for years, such enigmas occupied my child mind, but it wasn't for some time that I realized that these simple wonderments actually sit close to the base of much philosophical questioning.

These and related questions are native to the modern philosophical environment from which American evangelicalism sprang. So much so, in fact, that, arguably, to enjoy the fullest understanding of evangelicalism and its spirit requires an understanding of the philosophical structure of modernity. This is because evangelicalism was, in a very real sense, the Protestant Christian response to questions posed by the spirit of modernity. Thus, to approach an understanding of and appreciation for classical American

1. jbernal, "Is Philosophy," lines 12.

evangelicalism, we will need to look closely at the philosophical *zeitgeist* of modernity, into which evangelicalism was birthed.

Plato—Present at the Creation

Not surprisingly, seeking this understanding lands us back at Plato. It was the process philosopher Alfred North Whitehead himself who opined the epigraph to this chapter.

Without a doubt, the central icon in Plato's thought is his famous "Allegory of the Cave," according to which we are like prisoners in a cave, chained and facing a wall. On this wall dance shadows, cast from a fire burning behind us. Chained as we are, we cannot see the fire's flames, but only the light dancing in the shadows. For Plato, then, we exist in a shadow-land of furtive images—illusory reflections of reality. And thus, for Plato, the truly examined life consists of one's efforts to escape the cave and its shadowland of illusions to contemplate, unblinking, the light of the true and essential universal reality. Plato called this ultimate and essential reality the realm of ideas, or forms. Knowledge of this realm of reality was, for Plato, the highest calling.

Peter Kreeft, the Catholic philosopher, sums up Platonic thought by asserting that Plato's system suggests, "Order is not just our invention, our minds imposing structure and meaning, but that it's really there—in everything. It's *discovered* rather than invented."[2] This Platonic system, argues Kreeft, led to a structure of Hellenic thought that arguably set the philosophical tone down to the dawn of the modern era, with its revolution in rationalism and scientific advances.

Richard Tarnas, the intellectual historian, sums up the tenets of the Platonic system:

1. The world is an ordered cosmos, whose order is akin to an order within the human mind. A rational analysis of the empirical world is therefore possible.

2. The cosmos as a whole is expressive of a pervasive intelligence that gives to nature its purpose and design, and this intelligence is directly accessible to human awareness if the latter is developed and focused to a high degree.

2. Kreeft, "Platonic," disc 1.

3. Intellectual analysis at its most penetrating reveals a timeless order that transcends its temporal, concrete manifestations. The visible world contains within it a deeper meaning, in some sense both rational and mythic in character, which is reflected in the empirical order but which emanates from an eternal dimension that is both source and goal of all existence.

4. Knowledge of the world's underlying structure and meaning entails the exercise of a plurality of human cognitive faculties—rational, empirical, intuitive, aesthetic, imaginative, mnemonic, and moral.

5. The direct apprehension of the world's deeper reality satisfies not only the mind but the soul: it is, in essence, a redemptive vision that is at once intellectually decisive and spiritually liberating.[3]

According to Platonic thought, the cosmos is ordered, as are our minds. Reality, therefore, is *discovered*, not invented. The phenomena we sense around us, and the order in which all has its place, is reflective of an essential reality beyond the shadowlands in which we currently dwell. This essential reality, explains Kreeft, is the heart of Platonism and is what the Greeks described as *Logos*. A Platonist, therefore, according to Kreeft, believes that

> reality has an internal order, an intelligibility, a system—that it makes sense.
>
> That order is not just our invention, our minds imposing structure and meaning, but that it's really there in everything. It's discovered rather than invented. Things are ordered because they have intelligible natures or essences. That primary question, 'What is it?' has real answers. Reality is intelligible to mind. Being is open to reason and reason is open to being.[4]

In the main, this philosophical understanding largely set the tone for human wonderment until the dawn of modernity. Apropos to our discussion, the mind of the church in the premodern age had been centered "in Revelation as it had been enshrined in Scripture, in that Revelation which affirmed the existence of a God Who holds His Being separate and beyond the world."[5]

---

3. Tarnas, *Passion*, 71.

4. Kreeft, disc 1.

5. Guardini, *End*, 7.

It is important to recognize a corollary of this affirmation, which is that this premodern philosophical understanding rested upon key assumptions that modernity would later subvert. First of these was that the cosmos was constructed around the fixed, central sphere of the earth. Second, that humankind was central, unique, and of utmost importance in the order of reality. This reality was regarded as existing as a given hierarchy, which was "law abiding," even though these "laws were moral and not mechanical."[6] Finally, and perhaps most central to this premodern philosophical paradigm was that a divine *telos* or purpose was assumed resident at its core. "The world was treated as a great allegory whose essential secret was its religious meaning, not its operation or its causes."[7] Within these premodern parameters, the church reigned, "gathering all things into an inexhaustible unity," a unity which breathed in the "rhythm of the ecclesiastical year,"[8] ordering even time and teleological destiny themselves.

But this stasis would not last. Professor Guardini describes this ebbing of the church age:

> The medieval picture of the world along with the cultural order which it supported began to dissolve during the fourteenth century. This process of dissolution continued throughout the fifteenth and sixteenth centuries. By the seventeenth century it was complete, and a new picture of reality dawned clearly and distinctly over Europe.[9]

The historian Paul Johnson echoes Guardini, viewing the medieval period as a "total society," and describes its dissolution as "the break-up of the harmonious world-order which had evolved in the Dark Ages, on a Christian basis."[10]

Premodernity and the "Era of the Church"

To further our understanding of modernity, it will help to first find our bearings by glancing back at its antecedent, creatively christened by scholars and historians as "premodernity." In attempting to bracket the premodern

6. Barbour, *Issues in Science*, 18.
7. Ibid., 19.
8. Guardini, *End*, 21.
9. Ibid., 28.
10. Johnson, *History of Christianity*, 188–91.

era into the timeline of history, one quickly discovers that its suggested beginning and end dates are fungible, depending upon the context and scholar referenced. The philosopher Stephen R. C. Hicks assigns premodernity its beginning and end dates as 400 AD and 1300 AD, respectively.[11] In this he echoes Bertrand Russell, or nearly so, as Russell identifies this as the "medieval period, which we may reckon from about A.D. 400 to about A.D. 1400."[12]

Russell coins this thousand-year premodern period the "Era of the Church," describing the thinking and philosophy of this period as "essentially the philosophy of an institution, namely the Catholic Church."

Writing in his *Postmodernizing the Faith*, Millard Erickson describes a central theme of the premodern period, which he suggests was the "belief that observable nature was not the whole of reality."[13] We are reminded again of Plato and his forms. Erickson amplifies this initial description by attributing to the premodern a consistent supernaturalism, or assumption of the existence of a god or gods.[14] Hicks contributes an inventory of the tenets or traits of the premodern mindset, viz., supernaturalism, mysticism, faith, an assumption of original sin, collectivism, altruism, feudalism, and in a word, medieval.[15]

The Methodist theologian Thomas Oden provides his own description of premodernity, and underscores that the period was patristic, medieval, and guided by the consensus of the seven ecumenical church councils.[16] Erickson adds to these by pointing to a belief in the observable, objective existence of the created order, along with "a belief in a correspondence theory of truth: propositions are true if they correctly describe the realities they purport to describe, false if they do not."[17] Perhaps most significantly, Erickson sees the premodern era as one in which the "understanding of reality was teleological."[18] What this indicates, suggests Erickson, is that in the premodern mind, the cosmos was a reality within which humans occupied a purposeful, significant, and meaningful role and place.

---

11. Hicks, *Explaining Postmodernism*, 8.

12. Russell, *History*, 301.

13. Erickson, *Postmodernizing the Faith*, 15.

14. Ibid., 15.

15. Hicks, *Explaining Postmodernism*, 8.

16. Oden, *After Modernity*, 48.

17. Erickson, *Postmodernizing the Faith*, 15.

18. Ibid., 15.

The Georgetown University philosopher Heath White describes the negative aspect of this premodern sense of belonging. Premoderns, according to White, were "not free in many of the senses we now recognize."[19] For the premoderns, their (modern) freedom (along with their growing sense of individuality) was to arrive, in stages, and gradually, courtesy of three world-changing agents: the Renaissance, beginning in the fifteenth century; the Reformation in the sixteenth; and the Age of Reason, or Enlightenment, commencing in the seventeenth. We will review each, and show how the advent of evangelicalism was their natural outcome.

The Renaissance as Birth Pangs of the Modern

If the initial birth pangs of the modern era can be traced to the revolution that was the Renaissance, it is Francesco Petrarch who was the attending midwife. A well-traveled man of letters of the fourteenth century, Petrarch took upon himself the task of rediscovering and mastering the works of ancient thinkers such as Virgil, Cicero, Homer, and Plato.[20] Indeed, Tarnas asserts that, in his rediscovery of the ancients and his evangelistic sharing of them with his contemporaries, Petrarch "began the re-education of Europe."[21]

Petrarch's gospel of the ancients landed on good soil and gave rise to a cadre of intellectuals who came to be called "humanists." The term "humanist," explains the historian Jacques Barzun, in his magisterial *From Dawn to Decadence*, was first used to describe the writers of the fourteenth and fifteenth centuries who "rejected parts of the immediate past in favor of the culture they perceived in the classics of ancient Rome."[22] Kenneth Scott Latourette explains that *renaissance* literally "means new birth, as though during the Middle Ages Europe had been dead and had now again become alive."[23] To be a humanist in the heady time of the Renaissance, then, was to embrace a radical shift in perspective. It was, according to Barzun, to begin taking the revolutionary step of dealing "with the affairs of the world in a man-centered way."[24] While familiar to our ears, this radically new posture

19. White, *Postmodernism 101*, 26.

20. Tarnas, *Passion*, 209.

21. Ibid., 209.

22. Barzun, *From Dawn to Decadence*, 44.

23. Latourette, *History of Christianity*, 604.

24. Barzun, *From Dawn to Decadence*, 44.

stood in stark contrast to the spirit of the medieval age—an age in which, as Guardini has described, the cosmological picture of the world assumed the *Logos* as the "external exemplar of the world," and provided "a harmony whose meaning was eternal" and in which "history was fixed."[25]

Tarnas also notes that at about this time numerous significant technical inventions occurred, serving as catalysts to this adventuresome and heroic spirit. These included the magnetic compass, gunpowder, the mechanical clock, and the printing press. Together, these inventions began to reward humanity with a mastery of the world around them, "separating and freeing the structure of human activities from the dominance of nature's rhythms."[26]

This new age or era, explains Latourette, was one in which "the men of the Renaissance took pleasure in nature and sought to explore and understand it."[27] It was, he continues, an age in which humans were "self-confident, believing in themselves and man. They took joy in their critical faculties, and especially in challenging what had been accepted in the Middle Ages. They poured scorn on scholasticism and the school men."[28]

In summation, the Renaissance should be considered as a precursor to the advent of the modern and the harbinger of a number of critical changes. First, it shifted people's focus from the heavenlies to earthly concerns. Second, central to that focus was the increased attention paid to the consideration of humanity itself. Third, the life of the mind and intellectual pursuits expanded out beyond the matters of the church and the spiritual. Next, it was a time of rapid technological advances, and, as if to encapsulate all the above, the Renaissance ushered in a surge in the self-confidence in what it meant to be human.

Finally, even while underscoring the importance of both Petrarch and the Renaissance, Russell cautions, "The Renaissance was not a popular movement; it was a movement of a small number of scholars and artists."[29] It fell upon another priest, Martin Luther, to usher in the onslaught of more wide-ranging, democratic change, in the form of the Reformation.

---

25. Guardini, *End*, 31.
26. Tarnas, *Passion*, 225.
27. Latourette, *History of Christianity*, 604.
28. Ibid., 605.
29. Ibid.

Luther—A Crisis of Faith and a Reformation

Phyllis Tickle, the amanuensis—or at least herald—of what has come to call itself the "emerging church" or "emerging conversation," proposes perhaps a slightly reductionist, though helpful, synopsis of Luther's protest. She concludes, "All Luther did on October 31, 1517, was say, 'Look, there's a hole!' followed by the observation, 'We're shipping water here, folks.'"[30] In good humor and postmodern fashion, Tickle wonders aloud whether October 31, 1517, truly was the date on which Luther changed the world by pounding his 95 Theses to the front door of All Saints Church in Wittenberg—or if said church even featured a front door. Regardless, she provides an excellent synopsis of the effects of Luther's pounding by stating that when he did so, he began "the process of wrenching, deconstructing, liberating, anxiety-producing, world-rending change as it works its way, straight as the proverbial arrow, from one regimen for ordering life to a new and unprecedented one."[31]

Luther was born on November 11, 1483. The historian Roland Bainton humorously suggests, "the reform that was to convulse Christendom was initiated by a Catholic monk and priest interested only in reforming himself."[32] Initially, Luther was uninterested in reform of any sort, and presumably theology of any kind, launched as he was by his ambitious father on a trajectory of legal studies. Luther was an excellent student, with a flair for the dramatic, and in July 1505 he experienced a dramatic and life changing event that altered his life—and ours—forever. Latourette reports of Luther that while out walking one "sultry summer day, a bolt of lightning felled him and, in terror of death, he called on St. Anne for help and made a vow to become a monk."[33] The storm passed, Luther was saved, but his budding legal career sacrificed. True to his vow, Luther entered the Augustinian monastery at Erfurt and commenced his study of theology with the priesthood as his goal. Though ordained as a priest in 1507, holy orders afforded Luther little consolation. Bainton reports that Luther "was one of those medieval Christians who took very seriously the 'four last things'—death, judgment, heaven and the eternal fire."[34] Luther could not bring himself to find easy accommodation with his tortured spirituality

30. Tickle, *Great Emergence*, 43.
31. Ibid., 17.
32. Bainton, *Christendom*, 8.
33. Latourette, *History of Christianity*, 705.
34. Bainton, *Christendom*, 9.

and his understanding of the ultimate things. Despite fasting, mortifications, and regular and lengthy confessions, Luther found little peace, and suffered periods of acute depression. The event that ultimately pushed him over the edge was the occasion of his first Mass celebrated as a newly ordained priest. He did fine, until reaching the awesome words of the Mass in which he was to solemnly intone, "We offer unto thee the living, the true, the eternal God." He later related that

> At these words I was utterly stupefied and terror-stricken. I thought to myself, with what tongue shall I address such majesty, seeing that all men ought to tremble in the presence of even an earthly prince? Who am I, that I should lift up my eyes or raise my hands to the divine majesty? The angels surround him. At his nod the earth trembles, and shall I, a miserable little pygmy, say, "I want this, I ask for that?" For I am dust and ashes and full of sin, and I am speaking to the living, the eternal, and the true God.[35]

Indeed. But despite, or perhaps owing to, his intensity, spiritual relief was to come slowly to Luther, only gradually manifesting as the monk was teaching out of St. Paul's letters to the Romans and the Galatians. It was here that the impact of Paul's teaching that "the just shall live by faith" hit the struggling priest with full force. For Luther, if our salvation was of faith, then it was *completely* of faith, and faith alone. Indeed, it was *sola fide*. It is not insignificant that by embracing this degree of *personal* and *individual* understanding of spirituality, Luther and the other reformers initiated the process of plucking themselves from the medieval stream of tradition, firmly dropping themselves into the rapids of a new era—the modern era. As Brown explains, "the intense debates caused by the Reformers' understanding of justification by faith shifted the focus away from metaphysical analysis and speculation and onto personal experience and the role of Scripture in the believer's knowledge of God."[36]

We can detect in this emphasis on *personal* experience, the influence of Petrarch and his Renaissance humanism. Tarnas concurs, though commenting from a more historical and sociological (rather than theological) perspective:

> Perhaps the most fundamental element in the genesis of the Reformation was the emerging spirit of rebellious, self–determining individualism and particularly the growing impulse for intellectual

35. Ibid., 9.
36. Brown, *Christianity*, 145.

and spiritual independence, which had now developed to that crucial point where a potently critical stand could be sustained against
the West's highest cultural authority, the Roman Catholic Church.[37]

If one wonders why it took the Reformation to begin seriously loosen-
ing the era's ties to the medieval mindset, Dean Inge has a simple, compelling answer: "The great Reformers were fighters."[38] This being so, perhaps
especially in Luther's case, it did not take long for his pugilistic urges to
crash headlong into the unfortunate decadence of the church of his day.
His first collision was with the then widespread practice of indulgences.
The selling of indulgences was a practice of fundraising that had monetary,
political, ecclesial, and purportedly spiritual implications. The questionable
practice arguably arrived at its profit-generating zenith just at the time Luther entered center stage. The Dominican priest John Tetzel, promoting the
indulgences, and being a better marketer, apparently, than biblical exegete,
created the pithy tag line to promote their sale:

> As soon as the coin in the coffer rings,
> The soul from purgatory springs.[39]

Though it played well in some quarters, the entire indulgence debacle
wreaked havoc with Luther's sense of both spiritual and ecclesial propriety,
not to mention biblical understanding. His response was to take his now
famous step of proposing his 95 Theses or Disputations on the Power of
Indulgences. The date, historians agree, was October 31, 1517, postmodern
skepticism notwithstanding. In posting his protest, Luther contested the
church on numerous points, in addition to his railing against the selling of
indulgences. He denied the ultimate authority of the pope and the councils, claiming that they could, in fact, err. He insisted that the Scriptures
alone constituted the ultimate authority, and thus the new doctrine of *sola
scriptura* was born. Finally, Luther conceded that while he himself might
theoretically be capable of error, he would not admit to such unless, by the
power of plain reason, he could be shown to be out of step with what he
viewed as the clear intent of the Scriptures.[40]

To Protestant ears, even at the ebb of the modern era, such a bold
assertion lacks the jarring impact it would have held for the hearers in

---

37. Tarnas, *Passion*, 234.
38. Inge, *Platonic Tradition*, 37.
39. Bainton, *Christendom*, 15.
40. Latourette, *History of Christianity*, 709.

Luther's day. Indeed, Luther's Theses ignited a firestorm, and as Bainton underscores, the Lutheran discussion quickly metastasized from one focused on indulgences to a more significant consideration of authority. Simply: who, now, was in charge? To even imagine and give voice to such questions constituted a break with the medieval mind, and was in itself a characteristically modern act in that it implied that the *individual*—rather than any institution—might in fact be the ultimate seat of decision-making power. Courtesy of Luther's protest, medieval humanity had taken another significant step toward the freedom and even license humanity would ultimately, fully realize in modernity.

The church and civil leaders opposing Luther struck on January 3, 1521, when the pope issued a bull of excommunication against him. Luther was hauled before the Diet at Worms, where he was urged to recant his writings and teachings. It was here that Luther gave his iconic defense, in which he repeated that

> His conscience was captive to the word of God and that unless he were convicted by Scripture and plain reason, for he did not accept the authority of Popes and councils since they had contradicted one another, he would not recant anything. To do so would be neither right nor safe . . . here I stand, I cannot do otherwise.[41]

This left little doubt as to where Luther stood on the issues of indulgences, papal authority, Tradition, the perspicuity of Scriptures and the efficacy and centrality of the individual in one's own soteriological process. In Luther's eyes, individuals were now responsible for working out their own salvation—by faith and via the plain and reasonable understanding of Holy Scriptures. Tarnas asserts, "The Reformation was a new and decisive assertion of rebellious individualism—of personal conscience, of 'Christian liberty,' of critical private judgment against the monolithic authority of the institutional Church, and, as such, further propelled the Renaissance's movement out of the medieval Church and medieval character."[42]

It is an interesting thought exercise to ask ourselves whether Luther had any idea as to the landslide he would ultimately initiate as he struggled to dislodge and roll the twin boulders of *sola fide* and *sola scriptura* down the hill and into the heart of the sixteenth century. Erasmus, Luther's contemporary and one-time friend, remained loyal to the authority of the

41. Ibid., 717.
42. Tarnas, *Passion*, 239.

church, cautioning that, since some Scriptures were obscure, Luther's approach could lead to an excess of private and individual interpretations. Luther, reports Bainton, insisted there was no problem and, instead, sought to soothe Erasmus' fears, holding "that the Spirit would lead all responsive hearts to a common judgment."[43] Armed with the advantage of five hundred years of Protestant history, we might, in this case, judge Erasmus the more insightful and forward thinking. In any case, once Luther struck his blow for individualism, liberty of conscience, the catholic accessibility of the Holy Scriptures, and the universal priesthood of all believers, who, exactly, was to be in charge?

It is important to note that Luther's proposals took root at the close of one age—the medieval—and the dawning of the next—the modern. As Luther's theology gained ascendancy, established ecclesial authority was eclipsed and Protestantism was born. Similarly, many Protestant thinkers and theologians suggest that we are now living at the close of the modern age, with the question of authority being asked once again. Roger Olson, a central figure in the current lobby for evangelical change, offers solace in his iconically titled manifesto, *Reformed and Always Reforming*. He reminds his readers that current "reformers" should recognize that their protests are not without precedent, and that those so protesting should find comfort in remembering of Luther that "his reforming efforts were countered with accusations that he was destroying the church by questioning its absolute authority and monopoly on truth."[44]

Tickle, too, recognizing the momentousness of Luther's landslide, also asks, "Where now is the authority?" and then proceeds to answer her own question: "*Sola scriptura. Sola scriptura.*"[45] But Tickle doesn't stop there and insightfully looks downstream, past Luther's negation of the absoluteness of the pope, the councils, the magisterium, and the clerics, and notes a likely unintended consequence of the Lutheran revolt. "A more long-range benefit of the Reformation's placing ultimate authority in Scripture was that, when coupled with the principle of the priesthood of all believers, *sola scriptura* required absolute and universal literacy if it were going to work."[46] And work it did. Fueled by the relatively new technology of movable type, it rendered books, including Luther's own translation of the New

43. Bainton, *Christendom*, 25.
44. Olson, *Reformed*, 88.
45. Tickle, *Great Emergence*, 45.
46. Ibid., 46.

Testament from Greek into German, affordable to wide markets. At last, every German from blacksmith to scholar had the tools needed to assume his own individual and personal priesthood. Tickle observes that this widespread literacy was not without greater effect, and "in turn accelerated the drive toward rationalism and from there to Enlightenment and from there straight into the science and technology and literature and governments that characterize our lives today."

The point here is that Luther and the Reformers successfully staked out territory beyond the dominance of the church territory, where human rationality was its own governor and empirical encounter with the natural world was now possible. Therefore, for increasingly modern minds, "the world could now be analyzed not according to its assumed sacramental participation in static divine patternings . . . but rather according to its own distinct dynamic material processes, devoid of direct reference to God and his transcendent reality."[47]

The Renaissance and the Reformation Yield the Glimmer of the Enlightenment and Advent of the Modern Era

This radical reorientation of the human gaze and focus was now to come to full flower in the next historical iteration, which has come to be known as the Age of Reason or, simply, the Enlightenment.

As we have already seen, the three forces of the Renaissance, the Reformation, and the Age or Reason or Enlightenment worked as a confluence that yielded the modern age and mind. Also, as we have already seen, Tarnas makes the point that the Reformation's work was, in part, to restore a "predominantly biblical theology against a Scholastic theology (which) helped to purge the modern mind of Hellenic notions . . . thereby supporting the development of a new science of nature."[48]

With the advent of this new mind, God may still have been in his heaven, but as to the earth, and nature, both were now fair game for humanity's rational observation, management, and even control. With the closing of the Era of the Church, the world could effectively be described as "disenchanted." Tarnas describes the radical shift this disenchantment represents by explaining, "To assume, as did the ancient and medieval philosophers, that the world was divinely permeated and ordered in a manner

47. Tarnas, *Passion*, 241.
48. Ibid., 241.

directly accessible to the human mind, leading the mind directly to God's hidden purposes, was to bar the mind from insight into nature's actual forms."[49] The Enlightenment, then, was largely the story of humanity's feeling itself increasingly free to directly observe, measure, experiment with, and exercise increasing control over nature.

Ernst Cassirer, long considered an Enlightenment authority, proposes that it is the spirit of Descartes that sets the tone for *all* things Enlightenment. "After the middle of the seventeenth century the Cartesian spirit permeates all fields of knowledge until it dominates not only philosophy, but also literature, morals, political science and sociology, asserting itself even in the realm of theology to which it imparted a new form."[50]

Henry May notes the challenge of strictly defining the Enlightenment, observing that if optimism is included in the definition, Voltaire, Hume, and others will necessarily be excluded. Conversely, if an attempted definition focuses too ardently on rationalism itself, then Hume and Rousseau would not make the cut. He cleverly suggests a solution, holding that his study is thus "not about the Enlightenment *and* religion, but rather about the Enlightenment *as* religion."[51] He continues, providing a helpful description: "the Enlightenment consists of all those who believe two propositions: first, that the present age is more enlightened than the past; and second, that we understand nature and man best through the use of our natural faculties."[52]

Having set worthy expectations for our achieving a general understanding of the Enlightenment, while recognizing that a detailed review is beyond the scope and purpose of this study, let us turn, nonetheless, to an overall review of the Enlightenment. To begin, we will first consider the one man whose thought, perhaps more than any other, provided the philosophical underpinning for the period of human history we now call the Enlightenment.

Rene Descartes . . . Ideas Do Have Consequences

Rene Descartes, born in 1596, may have had more to do with the ultimate shaping of modern philosophy than any other thinker. So suggests Arthur Holmes, who also proposes that Descartes' influence results from his

49. Ibid., 274.
50. Cassier, *The Philosophy*, 28.
51. May, *Enlightenment*, xiii.
52. Ibid., xiv.

having "devised a new philosophic method modeled on mathematical reasoning, in order to build a philosophical system scientifically rather than perpetuating the speculative preconceptions of Scholasticism."[53] According to Bertrand Russell, Descartes set about to construct a system of thought based upon what Russell describes as "Cartesian doubt." Russell explains that to do so Descartes first determined to doubt everything possible. This radical doubt included Descartes' skepticism as to the trustworthiness of the senses. It also rendered impossible Descartes' reliance on mathematics. And while Descartes' doubt even undermined his faith in sensual perception, there remained, for Descartes, one reality that he could *not* doubt. For Descartes, thought was beyond doubt. Russell quotes Descartes' central apology for his philosophical system:

> While I wanted to think everything false, it must necessarily be that I who thought was something; and remarking that this truth, *I think therefore I am*, was so solid and so certain that all the most extravagant suppositions of the skeptics were incapable of upsetting it, I judged that I could receive it without scruple as the first principle of the philosophy that I sought.[54]

To this all-important bedrock in Descartes' philosophical system, Collin Brown adds a second major element—this being Descartes' effort to rationally support the existence of God as the ultimate and perfect being. Finally, Brown suggests a third element in Cartesian thought: Descartes' belief that there were "two kinds of reality; the mental and the material . . . on account of these two types of reality Descartes's thought is often described as dualistic."[55]

While these three principles may not strike us moderns (or postmoderns) as world-changing, in fact they were. But they were not without an important and truly earth-shattering philosophical precedent. This precedent can be found in the thought of a Franciscan monk who did his work in the fourteenth century.

William of Ockham was a theologian whose thought is now regarded as catalytic of what is now called "nominalism." Copleston, the Jesuit philosopher, suggests that "one of Ockham's main preoccupations as a philosopher was to purge Christian theology and philosophy of all traces of Greek necessitarianism, particularly of the theory of essences, which in

---

53. Holmes, *Christian Philosophy*, 42.

54. Russell, *History*, 64.

55. Brown, *Christianity*, 182.

his opinion endangered the Christian doctrines of the divine liberty and omnipotence."[56] According to Ockham, then, there is no essential reality beyond the firelight flickers of Plato's Cave. There are no forms. Weaver is more pointed in his evaluation of Ockhamist thought and its effects:

> It was William of Occam who propounded the fateful doctrine of nominalism, which denies that universals have a real existence . . . the issue ultimately involved is whether there is a source of truth higher than, and independent of man . . . the practical result of nominalist philosophy is to banish the reality which is perceived by the intellect and to posit as reality that which is perceived by the senses.[57]

Here, Ockhamist and Cartesian thought can be seen working together to yield what the philosophy of science writer Ian Barbour describes as a "radical *dualism of matter and mind.*"[58]

At this point, the physical world and the cosmos increasingly came to be regarded as "self-sufficient matter extended in space,"[59] again, best encountered and understood through physics and mathematics. Thus, while Descartes ceded to the mind the territory of religion, he regarded all phenomena perceived by the senses as best understood and manipulated through the tools of physics and mathematics. For Descartes and those influenced by his thought, the cosmos and everything in it—including humankind—was best perceived as a machine and understood as mechanical in nature.

But the dimension of thought was not alone in reflecting Enlightenment changes. As if to anticipate the Cartesian model which would provide the philosophical foundation for modern science, a number of late-Renaissance thinkers had already begun to question the validity of the medieval concept of the universe. The three thinkers/scientists who would most effectively question this medieval cosmology were Copernicus, Galileo, and Newton.

Prior to the arrival of Copernicus (b. 1473), the medieval world had subscribed to what is known as the Ptolemaic model of the cosmos. This was a model based on Greek and medieval science in which humanity not only resided at the center of the cosmos, but even more importantly, this central position reflected its ultimate purpose or destiny. According

56. Copleston, *History*, vol. 3, 48.

57. Weaver, *Ideas Have Consequences*, 3.

58. Barbour, *Issues in Science*, 28.

59. Ibid., 28.

THEOSIS

to medieval cosmology and theology, "man was unique and central in both location and importance.[60] This was the worldview with which the Copernican calculations of the cosmos collided. In short, Copernicus, the astronomer and mathematician, took the revolutionary step of positing a heliocentric model of the solar system. By mathematically testing his revolutionary thesis—relegating the earth to an orbiting rather than central role—Copernicus discovered that the planets' orbits made more sense, and seemed to function more smoothly and predictably. Ultimately, with the assault of Copernican calculations, the aging Ptolemaic paradigm simply collapsed, and the earth could no longer be seen as being at the center of the solar system. But this collapse was not without its collateral damage to the medieval mind. Along with this downgrading of the earth and its assumptive place in the cosmic hierarchy came the logical corollary that humankind was not as central as historically presumed. If this were so, then perhaps humankind's teleology and destiny were also in need of a down-grading. Life was just life, death just death, and perhaps the universe no longer deserved being "treated as a great allegory whose essential secret was its religious meaning."[61]

Following Copernicus, Galilei Galileo (b. 1564) was unique in that he not only *thought* new thoughts, but, armed with his telescope, he actually conducted physical experiments designed to prove or disprove his new hypotheses. For this, Galileo has been called the father of modern science. But that's not all he was called. For his trouble, he was also called before the Inquisition and condemned to house arrest, his ideas judged contrary to church teaching.[62] With Galileo, that

> teleological explanation, characteristic of earlier thought, had given way to descriptive explanation, best summarizes the most significant effect of Galilean thought. Galileo asked not *why* objects fall but *how* they fall. He was content to describe how phenomena progress, completely ignoring questions about the purposes they serve.[63]

By employing observation and experimentation, followed by model building, Galileo had shifted thought and inquiry and set the foundations for a new paradigm. Russell describes this shift as the genesis of the scientific method, and the point at which thinkers began to systematically

60. Ibid., 18.
61. Ibid., 19.
62. White, *Postmodernism 101*, 29.
63. Barbour, *Issues in Science*, 26.

28

"reach principles inductively from observation of particular facts," and also the point at which this system of thought "replaced the Hellenic belief in deduction from luminous axioms derived from the mind of the philosopher."[64] Indeed, with Galileo, the ground shifted, and though he "saw no fundamental contradiction between science and faith,"[65] the die was cast and would change forever the way in which theology, philosophy, and science were regarded.

The final member of our paradigm-shifting trinity of giants of thought was Isaac Newton. "Modernity," proposes Stanley Grenz, "was born out of an intellectual revolution. The specifically scientific dimension of that revolution was sparked by Galileo (1564–1642) and reached its climax with Newton (1642–1727)."[66] It was at that zenith of thought that the laws of motion and gravity and a mechanical view of the universe were firmly established. Newton himself was a man of deep faith who saw no gulf between orthodox faith and this new, mechanical view of the cosmos. In fact, writing in the preface of his *Principia Mathematica*, Newton maintained that his gravitational theory buttressed the belief in a deity. In fact, suggested Newton, this deity, was "the most perfect mechanic of all."[67] Voltaire, another Enlightenment giant, considered Newton the greatest man who ever drew breath. And why not? According to Tarnas, Newton's "achievement was celebrated as the triumph of the modern mind over ancient and medieval ignorance. Newton had revealed the true nature of reality."[68] Tarnas summarizes,

> The Newtonian-Cartesian cosmology was now established as the foundation for a new world view. By the beginning of the eighteenth century, the educated person in the West knew that God had created the universe as a complex mechanical system . . . The Scientific Revolution—and the birth of the modern era—was now complete.[69]

It is against this backdrop and confluence of intellectual forces that the evangelical movement was born.

64. Russell, *History*, 39.

65. Brown, *Christianity*, 176.

66. Grenz, *Primer*, 48.

67. Brown, *Christianity*, 218.

68. Tarnas, *The Passion*, 270.

69. Ibid., 271.

3

The Marriage of Modernity
and Evangelicalism

Modernity—Its Definition and Its Place
on the Timeline of the Human Story

IN HIS HELPFUL BOOK *A Primer on Postmodernism*, Stanley Grenz sets plausible brackets for the modern age. He suggests that modernism was birthed following a long gestation period, and muses that "the Renaissance was a grandmother of modernity, and the Enlightenment was its true mother."[1] If this is so, then the Enlightenment itself, which Grenz brackets from 1650 to 1800, lasted for less than two hundred years before yielding to the modern age, "which now," he concludes, "seems to be in its twilight stage."[2] In *The Challenge of Postmodernism*, David Dockery posits a similar dating. "The easiest way to identify the time span or epoch of modernity is as this precise 200-year period between 1789 and 1989, between the French Revolution and the collapse of Communism."[3]

Having identified the modern period as this near two-hundred-year span, its closing nearly concurrent with the twilight of the exhausted and blood-baptized twentieth century, we can now catalog the tenets of this modern period.

1. Grenz, *Primer*, 60.
2. Ibid., 60.
3. Dockery, *Challenge*, 23.

If there is any living theologian who might credibly serve as an icon of the truly modern theologian, it is likely Thomas Oden, who describes himself as a classical "Movement Theologian." His activism afforded him a front row seat on nearly innumerable bandwagons, including the early ecumenical movement, the civil rights struggles, the labor movement, engagement with the ACLU, forays into Gestalt therapy, and more. Many more.[4] As an iconic "modern" theologian, Oden's analysis of this modern period is especially "real time" and insightful. In his, *After Modernity . . . What?*, Oden defines "modern" as related to "*the modo*, the 'just now,' the most recent thing."[5] Oden identifies this modern ethos as "the overarching intellectual ideology of a historical period whose hegemony has lasted from the French Revolution to the present," characterized by "moral relativism, narcissistic hedonism, naturalistic reductionism, and autonomous individualism."[6] The modern era is also one, according to Oden, "which assumes that chronologically recent ways of knowing the truth are self-evidently superior to all premodern alternatives."[7]

It is important to note that while the Renaissance had resuscitated the respect for the ancients and their wisdom, modernity eschewed the classics and their wisdom, and instead lionized the "just now" and the "modern." In volume 3 of his *Systematic Theology*, Oden describes the modern spirit as

> an inveterate modern chauvinism that assumes that modern consciousness is intrinsically superior to all premodern modes of thinking; conversely, all premodern thinking is assumed to be intrinsically inferior to the modern consciousness. That premise is deeply ingrained in the pride of modernity.[8]

Finally, Oden catalogues the tenets or traits of the modern period, identifying them as "autonomous individualism, demystification, secularization, naturalistic reductionism [and] scientific empiricism."[9] Dockery echoes Oden: "the enchantment of modernity is characterized by technological messianism, enlightenment idealism, quantifying empiricism, and the smug fantasy of inevitable historical progress."[10]

4. Oden, *After Modernity*, 26.

5. Ibid., 43.

6. Ibid., 46.

7. Ibid., 46.

8. Oden, *Systematic Theology*, 379.

9. Oden, *After Modernity*, 48.

10. Dockery, *Challenge*, 24.

It is imperative to recall that the advent of the modern era was ushered in on the coattails of a radically new way of viewing the cosmos itself. As Tarnas explains,

> The Newtonian-Cartesian cosmology was now established as the foundation for a new world view. By the beginning of the eighteenth century, the educated person in the West knew that God had created the universe as a complex mechanical system, composed of material particles moving in an infinite neutral space according to a few basic principles, such as inertia and gravity that could be analyzed mathematically.[11]

Tarnas summarizes the effect of Newtonian physics on the emerging modern mind in a three-point synopsis. First:

> In contrast to the medieval Christian cosmos, which was not only created but continuously and directly governed by a personal and active, omnipotent God, the modern universe was now seen as an impersonal phenomenon, governed by regular and natural laws, and understandable in exclusively physical and mathematical terms.[12]

Second:

> Science replaced religion as preeminent intellectual authority, as definer, judge, and guardian of the cultural world view. Human reason and empirical observation replaced theological doctrine and scriptural revelation as the principal means for comprehending the universe.[13]

And finally,

> The Christian dualistic stress on the supremacy of the spiritual and transcendent over the material and concrete was now largely inverted, with the physical world becoming the predominant focus for human activity . . . The Christian dualism between spirit and matter, God and world, was gradually transformed into the modern dualism of mind and matter, man and cosmos: a subjective and personal human consciousness versus an objective and impersonal material world.[14]

11. Tarnas, *Passion*, 270, 271.
12. Ibid., 285.
13. Ibid., 286.
14. Ibid., 286.

This dualism both echoes and was the logical conclusion of what the physicist and science writer Fritjov Capra identifies as a greater Cartesian dualism between mind (or spirit) and matter. Capra suggests that while the Newtonian world-as-machine paradigm allowed for a creator, as Newtonian science matured, spirit and the divine were gradually crowded out from the picture. But this new and modern "objective description of nature" was not only to become the ideal of science, but was also to guide the concept of knowing itself. This epistemological shift was to have a significant impact on how humans increasingly perceived the business of acquiring knowledge. Grenz offers his observation:

> Throughout the modern era, intellectuals in many disciplines have turned to the reasoning subject rather than divine revelation as the starting point for knowledge and reflection. Even modern theologians felt constrained to build on the foundation of rationalistic philosophy. They, too, accepted the primacy of reason advocated by Descartes . . . In the end, modern theologians ended up following Descartes's lead rather than trying to swim against the surge generated by the Age of Reason.[15]

For a growing number of early modern thinkers, God became "an unnecessary hypothesis."[16] Barzun echoes this spirit of the new modern age by asserting that as the new modern mind gained ascendancy, "God went into respected retirement."[17] Peter Berger, the sociologist of knowledge, explains that with the advent of modernity a pall of what he describes as "functional rationality" descended upon the modern mind. According to Berger, this "functional rationality means, above all, the imposition of rational controls over the material universe, over social relations and finally over the self."[18] The ascendancy of modernity, then, was marked both by a suspicion of the spiritual and by the rising hegemony of rationality. It was this nascent modern age into which evangelicalism was birthed.

15. Grenz, *Primer*, 65, 66.

16. Ibid., 65–66.

17. Barzun, *From Dawn to Decadence*, 271.

18. Berger, *Homeless Mind*, 202.

Evangelicalism and the Enlightenment—A Symbiotic Genesis

Garry Williams, contributing a chapter to *The Advent of Evangelicalism*, and referencing the historian David Bebbington, flatly asserts that evangelicalism was not simply affected by the Enlightenment, but was actually its offspring. He also offers his thesis of a direct linkage between the evangelical doctrine of salvific assurance and Enlightenment confidence.

> The activism of the Evangelical movement sprang from its strong teaching of assurance. That, in turn, was a product of the confidence of the new age about the validity of experience. The Evangelical version of Protestantism was created by the Enlightenment.[19]

The importance of this crucial factor of assurance cannot be overestimated when one considers the heritage of evangelicalism. As Williams explains, it was this assurance that differentiated the new evangelical movement from its predecessors, the Puritans. While the Puritans "had held that assurance is rare, late and the fruit of struggle in the experience of believers, the evangelicals believed it to be general, normally given at conversion and the result of simple acceptance of the gift of God."[20] This assurance yielded, as Williams explains, the "robust confidence" of the evangelicals, contrasted to the "introspective gloom" that had dogged the Puritans.[21] Assurance, confidence, optimism, and dynamism—theologically and culturally identifiable evangelical traits, to be sure—were also traits shared by the enthusiastic new moderns anticipating a world of infinite progress and opportunities.

Bebbington cites Jonathan Edwards as a pivotal figure in early evangelicalism and its evolution away from its Puritan roots toward an epistemic confidence in the assurance of one's own salvation. In his *Evangelicalism in Modern Britain*, Bebbington queries this Edwardian assurance.

> How could he be so bold? It was because he was far more confident than his Puritan forefathers of the powers of human knowledge. A person, he held, can receive a firm understanding of spiritual things through a 'new sense' which is as real as sight or smell.[22]

19. Haykin and Stewart, *Advent*, 347.
20. Ibid., 348.
21. Ibid., 348.
22. Ibid., 349.

Williams claims that Edwards could embrace this confidence largely due to his having drunk "deeply from the waters of the English Enlightenment, in particular from the works of John Locke . . . to put it simply, where Locke's empiricism said, 'you can trust your senses,' Edwards counseled, 'you can trust your spiritual sense.'"[23] This natural linkage shouldn't surprise, especially as we remind ourselves of E. L. Mascall's caution of nearly fifty years ago: "Christians themselves, however well instructed and thoughtful they may be, inevitably share in the intellectual climate and perspective of their time, even if they are conscious that it is, in one way or another, uncongenial to their faith."[24]

This nascent uncongeniality between the tenets of modernity and Christian orthodoxy would evolve over time, but in these early days the collegiality seemed nearly complete. And even as younger evangelicals would eventually come to blame the Enlightenment for the "kind of rationalism that, step by step, squeezes God out of the world,"[25] in these early days such was not the case. Indeed, the synergy between early evangelicalism and the Enlightenment was such that the historian Bebbington could actually propose that "far from being intrinsically opposed to one another, eighteenth-century evangelicalism has close ties to the Enlightenment and should actually be considered its creation."[26] This is a startling thesis largely because if Bebbington—perhaps *the* outstanding historian of evangelicalism—can rightly assert that evangelicalism was the "creation" of the Enlightenment, it follows that to most fully understand evangelicalism we must also understand the Enlightenment.

Mark Noll, Professor of Christian Thought at Wheaton College, describes the impact of the Enlightenment thinkers on the American Republic. He asserts that they worked hard to restore intellectual confidence to the inventory of Enlightenment ideals.

> They achieved these goals by arguing that all humans possessed, by nature, a common set of capacities—both epistemological and ethical—through which they could grasp the basic realities of nature and morality. Moreover, these human capacities could be studied as scientifically as Newton studied the physical world.[27]

23. Ibid., 349.
24. Mascall, *Secularization*, 1.
25. Haykin and Stewart, *Advent*, 30.
26. Ibid., 40.
27. Noll, *Scandal*, 85.

Not surprisingly, this above has a ring of optimism about it, along with a fairly sunny outlook as to the nature of the human condition, and as such runs counter to what we traditionally recognize as the revivalist thought of Edwards, Whitefield, et al. Noll asserts that this optimistic view of humanity had, by the early nineteenth century, become "a widely accepted assumption of America's evangelicals."[28] Noll also suggests that the Americans' quick and easy adoption of the tenets of the Enlightenment was accomplished principally for pragmatic reasons. By proposing legitimacy to the rationality of the "common man," Enlightenment thought provided the American Everyman with the fulcrum needed to topple powers such as royalty, inheritance, and tradition itself. Indeed, Enlightenment thought empowered the common man by identifying in him legitimacy and honor heretofore granted only to kings and rulers. Noll elaborates, pointing out that in their embrace of Enlightenment thought, early Americans were placing their confidence in objectivity, the preeminence of scientific inquiry, and the "common sense" of "self-evident truths," the "unalienable rights" of men and women and the obvious "laws of nature." Indeed, claims Noll, "Evangelical commitment to this form of the Enlightenment became deeply engrained, not only because it was so successful, but also because it was so intuitive, so instinctual, so much of second nature."[29]

Notably, the early evangelical embrace of Enlightenment principles produced both apologetical and theological fruit. Claims Noll, "Examples of apologetics grounded on scientific rationality abounded in the early national period . . . rigorous empiricism became the standard for justifying belief in God, revelation, and the Trinity . . . it also provided a key for using physical science itself as a demonstration of religious truths."[30]

Finally, Haykin summarizes Bebbington's thought by suggesting that both the Enlightenment and evangelicalism were deeply permeated with the spirit of empiricism. This empiricism was built on an unwavering trust in a methodological acquisition of knowledge through observation, experimentation, and measurement, along with a faith that truths learned were universal, rational, applicable, and sensible to sensible people everywhere. Second, Enlightenment thought was optimistic and imbued with a deep faith in the natural progress of knowledge and humanity as a whole. Third, the Enlightenment and evangelical worldviews were uniquely pragmatic in

28. Ibid., 86.

29. Ibid., 88.

30. Ibid., 91.

character. Things were true because they worked, and if they worked they were likely true. Finally, suggests Bebbington, characteristic of Enlightenment optimism was a deep faith in the natural benevolence of humankind. And while this "faith" ran counter to the assumptive evangelical belief in the fallenness of humankind, true conversion, taught the evangelicals, would in fact yield a benevolence of the quality lauded by Enlightenment thought.[31] Noll summarizes the close relationship between the two movements:

> This evangelical embrace of the Enlightenment at the turn of the eighteenth century still remains extraordinarily important nearly two centuries later because habits of the mind that the evangelical Enlightenment encouraged have continued to influence contemporary evangelical life. Of those habits, the most important were a particular kind of commitment to objective truth and a particular "scientific" approach to the Bible.[32]

Evangelicalism Defined

Bebbington defines evangelicalism by describing four characteristics that have become recognized evangelical hallmarks, together called the Bebbington Quadrangle. The initial evangelical characteristic cited is *conversionism*. Evangelicals universally recognize all humans as being in need of God and of a spiritual conversion through faith in Jesus Christ. Second is *activism*. While evangelicals resist any notion of salvation through works, labor on behalf of the kingdom of God is highly valued. Traditionally, the apex of this activism has been seen as missions and evangelism—sharing the Plan of Salvation. The third trait of Bebbington's Quadrangle is that evangelicalism is traditionally *biblicist*. Simply, for evangelicals, the Bible rather than church councils or church tradition is regarded as the source and final authority related to God's revelation and his truth. Finally, evangelical tradition is *crucicentric*, which is to say that evangelicals see the cross of Jesus Christ as sitting at the center of the entire soteriological drama of God reaching out to his creation.[33]

31. Haykin and Stewart, *Advent*, 42–46.

32. Noll, *Scandal*, 83.

33. Bebbington, "Evangelical Christianity," 30.

A Monkey Trial, a Clash of World Views, and the Legacy of Fundamentalism

Having identified at least a sibling (if not parental) relationship between the Enlightenment and evangelicalism, along with referencing the Bebbington Quadrangle of evangelicalism (conversionism, activism, biblicism, and crucicentrism), we are now armed with a good working understanding of the origins and DNA of classical evangelicalism. But though our study makes no pretense of presenting a thorough history of evangelicalism, we cannot leave the story of its genesis and maturation without at least touching on a monkey trial and evangelicalism's passage through fundamentalism. Indeed, without doing so it is impossible to understand younger evangelicals' increasing disquiet with the evangelicalism of their fathers—especially if they detect therein a whiff of fundamentalism past. Let us at least touch on the fundamentalists, who themselves occupy a legitimate and important place in the evangelical family tree. George Marsden supplies a working definition of fundamentalism:

> "Fundamentalism" refers to a twentieth-century movement closely tied to the revivalist tradition of mainstream evangelical Protestantism that militantly opposed modernist theology and the cultural change associated with it. Fundamentalism shares traits with many other movements to which it has been related . . . But it has been distinguished most clearly from these by its militancy in opposition to modernism.[34]

The term *fundamentalist* itself is related to the publication between 1910 and 1915 of twelve paperbacks entitled *The Fundamentals*, edited by such standouts as the prominent evangelist and writer R. A. Torrey. *The Fundamentals* were designed to clearly lay out the fundamentals of the faith and thereby counteract the acidic damage done by "infidel professors in Chicago."[35]

But it wasn't just the infidel professors of Chicago University that presented challenges. They were simply one source of concern. Compounding the problem was the advent of troublesome items such as German higher criticism, Freudian psychology, rapidly spreading secularization, and most significantly, Darwinism. Interestingly, while we have already seen that, as the child (or at least sibling) of the Enlightenment, evangelicalism had

---

34. Marsden, "Fundamentalism," 215.
35. Marsden, *Fundamentalism*, 118.

embraced science and empiricism. In Darwinism, however, science seemed to turn on the faith. Even before the dawning of the new twentieth century, Christians—especially conservatives—quickly recognized that a worldview with evolution at its base could easily evolve into one in which God was no longer necessary.

Protestant Christians found themselves increasingly moving along two parallel tracks. The conservative track had its DNA traceable back to the revivalism of earlier Protestantism, while those on the more liberal track found modernism more to its liking. Finally, in the early 1920s the two tracks lurched out of parallel in a small town in Dayton, Tennessee. It was there that John Scopes, a young biology teacher, was brought to trial for teaching the theory of evolution. The entire nation watched as the ACLU rolled in Clarence Darrow to defend Mr. Scopes against the renowned barrister William Jennings Bryan. Curiously, Scopes was actually found guilty of the crime of teaching evolution, a conviction later overturned on a legal technicality.

From the conclusion of this juridical train wreck, the two Protestant tracks, liberal and conservative, were put irreparably out of alignment. Liberals went their way while the fundamentalists increasingly opted for a militant separatism. As Marsden points out, through the 1930s the term "evangelicalism" was not a term that was popularly used by either liberals or conservatives, and "What chiefly distinguished fundamentalism from earlier evangelicalism was its militancy toward modernist theology and cultural change."[36]

By the mid-1940s, however, the tenor began to change. Organizations that would later be regarded as iconically evangelical came into being, including Youth for Christ International and, later, Campus Crusade for Christ. But perhaps the most significant and world-changing incident in this entire series of events was the experience of a young fundamentalist wrestling with his faith, seeking a deeper authenticity. In October 1946 he ventured to England, attending an evangelistic service in which the British preacher Stephen Olford exhorted his audience, to "Be not drunk with wine, wherein is excess; but be filled with the Spirit." The young American responded, ultimately declaring, "My heart is so flooded with the Holy Spirit!" With these words, the young Billy Graham rose from his knees, his own life and the trajectory of evangelicalism forever changed.[37]

36. Marsden, *Understanding*, 66.
37. Randall, "Outgrowing," 108.

Though originally a product of fundamentalism, the young Graham launched a series of evangelistic crusades beginning in the late 1940s and extending through the 1950s, for which he would gain national and even world prominence. And while such crusades were a staple in a nation with a revivalist history, Graham's crusades diverged radically from the expected in one significant point. The young evangelist actively reached out to a multiplicity of Christian traditions as he planned and managed his multi-city crusades. This marked a significant change in the crusade business, as the local fundamentalist churches in any given city discovered they were invited to *share* sponsorship of their city's Billy Graham crusade with non-fundamentalist Christians.

As a reforming fundamentalist, Graham wasn't alone. Young theologian Carl F. Henry penned his clarion call for evangelicals to think deeply about what he perceived as problems and limitations of the fundamentalist tradition. With his *The Uneasy Conscience of Modern Fundamentalism*, published in 1947, Henry initiated what would grow into a tsunami of self-conscious evangelical publishing. At about this point, explains Marsden, the two spheres increasingly recognized their irreconcilable differences.

> In the aftermath of the resulting schism within the coalition, "fundamentalism" came to be a term used almost solely by those who demanded ecclesiastical separatism. They called their former allies "neo-evangelicals" . . . Others in the reforming group simply called themselves "evangelical," the term that eventually became common usage both for them and for the wider movement."

And so modern evangelicalism was born.

But even recounting and recognizing the successes of the Graham crusades up through even the 1960s doesn't get us to the present in the evangelical story. Again, our primary focus in this exercise is not to engage in an exhaustive history of evangelicalism, but rather to understand the broad sweep of the movement so as to better understand its present situation. By the time of the upheaval of the 1960s, the movement began to show signs of its numerous moving parts increasingly moving in counter directions. As Marsden explains, "Vietnam polarized everyone."[38] So while evangelicals such as Harold Lindsell were vociferous in their conservatism, other evangelicals were busy sprinting in the opposite direction.

As James Davison Hunter has presciently reflected on the dynamism of evangelicalism, "Orthodoxy, as it has been noted, is not just a theological

38. Marsden, *Understanding*, 74.

matter. It is a cultural matter as well.[39]" By the early 1970s Hunter could conclude, "at another level the traditions defining conservative Protestant-ism are eroding; at another level orthodoxy itself (broadly construed) is being redefined." Clearly, America and its values were changing, and so too was evangelicalism. As Harvey Cox once wrote, "People not only live within empires, the empires live within them."[40] As evangelicalism changed and matured, it would evidence three significant phenomena.

The Charismatics

First was the charismatic or neo-Pentecostal movement, which had its ori-gins in Van Nuys, California, in an Episcopal church pastored by Fr. Dennis Bennett. The *glossalia* movement, though having begun in the Episcopal church, soon spread through evangelical churches, from high to low, urban to rural. It was also the catalyst of a spontaneous and vigorous home church or Bible study movement. Like the evangelical surge of the mid-twentieth century, neo-Pentecostalism also generated a publishing explosion, with new magazines such as the slick, pandenominational *Trinity* magazine and later *Charisma* magazine. Likewise, Christian bookshelves soon sagged with newly minted charismatic tomes. The effects and presence of the char-ismatic movement within evangelicalism persists to the present.

The Jesus People

The second phenomenon to note is the Jesus People movement, also having its origins in southern California. Chuck Smith, founder of Calvary Cha-pel Costa Mesa, is universally regarded as the godfather of the movement. Pastor Chuck preached, ministered to, and filled his churches with disen-franchised youths who might have hesitated to enter the typical church of that era. And, given the bristling political and cultural camps of that day, these youths might have seen the welcome mats to these churches hurriedly withdrawn upon their approach. But at Calvary Chapel hippies, beards, and countercultural types were welcomed and even lionized. Curiously, despite the hip tone, contemporary music, and excitement that went along with the movement, in the main, the theology and biblical exegesis trended conservative, especially in the Calvary Chapel network. "Maranatha!" was

39. Hunter, *Evangelicalism*, 163.
40. Cox, *Future*, 71.

the movement's watchword, with the glorious return of Jesus expected at any moment. Like the charismatic movement, to which it was not wholly unrelated, the Jesus People movement's legacy lives on in numerous forms, including the Calvary Chapel system itself and also the Vineyard Movement, which grew from the Calvary network.

Church Growth and Management Principles

A third phenomenon of the evangelical movement in the second half of the twentieth century that should not go unmentioned is the church growth movement.

One of the single, most significant characteristics of the church growth movement is its conscious intentionality. That is to say, church growth proponents are conscious and intentional when it comes to recognizing and exploiting the mechanisms of modern management, leadership, and organizational theory to plant, grow, and sustain their churches. As one recent study reports, "Leaders of the modern church growth movement have articulated that churches need to be well-managed organizations, pursuing organizational excellence, and learning from the business sector."[41]

When one thinks of churches and their pastors learning from the business sector, the "disciple/guru" relationship spanning twenty-plus years shared by Rick Warren and his mentor, Peter Drucker, comes readily to mind. Drucker, the Vienna-born godfather of the discipline of modern business management, has rightly secured his place in the pantheon of American business greats. In a YouTube eulogy of his mentor, Warren relates his passion and affection for Drucker. "I didn't just admire him. I love this man. In my life I've had a number of different mentors in my life and Peter was one of those mentors."[42] Likewise, Bill Hybels, senior pastor of the megachurch Willow Creek Community Church, has enthused that the two men who have most shaped his thinking on matters like staff performance are "Jesus and Peter Drucker."[43]

Drucker, himself an Episcopalian, imparted nuggets of management and leadership wisdom, which Warren readily integrated into his leadership and ministry at his 15,000-member Saddleback Church. In their regular mentor-discipleship conclaves, the guru would reportedly query the

41. Davis et al., "Stale in the Pulpit?," 354.
42. Warren, "Rick Warren."
43. Maddox, "In the Goofy," 154.

pastor, "Don't tell me what you're doing, Rick. Tell me what you *stopped* doing."[44] That Drucker had been able to successfully identify and convey the principles of management and leadership to his disciples would seem to be borne out by the obvious success of megachurches like Warren's and Hybels'. Based on the numbers alone, it might be tempting to simply conclude that, whatever one might think of the church growth or megachurch phenomenon, it is certainly not possible to "argue with success"! And yet, if we are to buy into the embrace of business strategies for church growth, then one must go all the way, and ask a couple of key business questions of the church growth proponents. First, how should we define success? Is it sheer size of membership? Or is it something different? Influence? Legacy? Spirituality? This question is critical and it is related to a second, equally critical question. That is, as we employ business wisdom and strategies to grow and manage our megachurches, what business are we *really in*?

There are those studying the church growth and megachurch phenomena, the theologian and political philosopher Marion Maddox among them, who have second thoughts about the marriage of business and church. Maddox has suggested that "growth churches actively model their approach on global capitalist corporations, complete with entrepreneurial CEOs and top-down management. Their leaders are exemplars of charismatic, entrepreneurial visioning with a strict corporatism."[45] In Maddox's mind, when it comes to the evangelists of church growth, the missional envoys have gone native.

The sociologist John Hayward's attempt to create an ultra-modern model of church growth and decline might serve as an iconic underscoring of Maddox's point. Hayward attempts to forecast congregational growth or decline through a formula (a snippet of which is shown below) measuring the variable populations in a church: the unbelievers, the enthusiasts and the inactive believers, where $C = A + B$, the total population of the community. Hypothesizes Hayward, "Let ta be the average duration of the enthusiastic period, Ca be the number converted by one enthusiast during the whole of their enthusiastic period, and g be the fraction of converts who become enthusiasts . . ."[46]

$$dB = (1 - g) \, CaA + A$$
$$dt \, ta \, ta \, . \, . \, .$$

44. Karlgaard, "Peter Drucker."
45. Maddox, "In the Goofy," 154.
46. Hayward, "General Model," 182.

At this point, even those gifted with an affinity for both math and management might find themselves wondering if the pragmatism, rationalism, and business tools of high-modernity might possibly, at times, be misapplied (or overapplied) in the church context. And perhaps we can only marvel at the church's survival through its initial two millennia, unaided as it was, by church growth tools.

Whatever else might be said of the church growth and megachurch phenomena, a case might be made that it is the modern period, with its embrace of empirical and rational management and measurement tools, that could best give rise to such phenomena.

Even so, "success" aside, at the close of modernity, the evangelicals—especially the younger—found themselves increasingly disenchanted with such success. We will explore this disenchantment, but first there are two remaining phenomena of late-twentieth-century evangelicalism that deserve mention.

The Decade of the Evangelical— Evangelicals Realize Political Influence

The first of these was the surge of political involvement and influence the evangelicals enjoyed in the 1970s and 1980s, spearheaded by energetic actors, including Jerry Falwell, the Moral Majority, Pat Robertson, Christian Voice, the Religious Roundtable, and others. By 1976, Newsweek magazine had already declared that year "The Year of the Evangelical." It was a timely declaration. In that same year, one of Evangelicalism's own, the peanut farming Southern Baptist Jimmy Carter, won the White House.

Following Carter, Americans turned to a former B-movie actor straight out of the Wild West. Ronald Reagan seemed everything Carter was not. Reagan was optimistic, light-hearted, exuded an easily conveyed sense of right and wrong, and announced that it was "Morning in America again." Under the new President, the nation exited the Carter economic downturn, and the economy roared back to life. America, it seemed, was on a roll. So too were the political prominence, power, and prestige of the evangelicals. Hunter reports that by 1981 active supporters of the above-mentioned "religious right" groups had surged to an estimated "4 million laymen and 37,000 to 70,000 clergy."[47] The issues embraced by the newly politically influential evangelicals included abortion, the changing role

47. Hunter, *Evangelicalism*, 125.

of women in society and the church, homosexuality, and school prayer. Evangelicals were no longer reduced to simply fulminating on the sidelines. Pioneering and perfecting new technologies such as data-driven direct mail fundraising and forays into assorted electronic media provided the evangelicals with powerful platforms and large megaphones.

Even so, all was not well within evangelicalism. There were those—particularly the younger—who were beginning to question the tenor of the evangelicalism of the 1980s. Diana Butler Bass, a *Huffington Post* blogger, religious historian, and social commentator, has contributed her intriguingly personal encounter with the Reaganistic evangelicalism of the 80s. During the late 1970s Bass had been a young student at a West Coast Christian college. She recounts the excitement on campus during her years there, when a residence hall could organize itself around a cause and young coeds would wrestle with feminist tomes, pontificating late into the night. But reflecting upon her visit to the same campus ten years later, Bass relates with sadness that little American flags now decorated "flower arrangements in the dining hall," and in those same dorms where students had once conducted tête-à-tête on all manner of social issues, they now sat mesmerized before their monitors, testing their mettle against the latest video game adversaries. "What happened?" Bass queried a professorial colleague, forlornly. "Ronald Reagan," her associate sagely responded. Reagan had successfully "re-created a mythic American past, giving people a sense of security when things changed too quickly or when people feared the results of change." He concluded, "You cannot move forward with nostalgia." Opines Bass, "In 1980, in a close election, we opted to go back."[48] Perhaps, even now, it is too soon to conclude whether Bass's summation of the 1980s as regression will prove out. Perhaps she has, at least, proven in her woeful 1991 return to the Santa Barbara campus that Thomas Wolfe was right—you can't go home again.

As the 1980s came to a close, the political influence and reach of the evangelicals ebbed. As Martin Marty wrote at the close of that decade, this ebbing was hastened by the "fall or compromising of Jim Bakker, Oral Roberts, Jimmy Swaggart and a host of slightly lesser-known figures."[49] Marty then sagely observes of the evangelicals that "Increasingly, especially after some punishing public encounters, they are aware that, while their power is

48. Bass, *Christianity*, 226.
49. Marty, "Years," 173.

to be reckoned with, they will not run the show."[50] Indeed, Marty concludes his look at the evangelicals and their decade by wisely prognosticating that the coming "years cannot be the Years of the evangelicals in the same way the previous ones were. A period has ended. The evangelical renewal did not lead to general revival and harder times may be coming for all institutional forms of religion."[51] Indeed, revival did not follow, though arguably those harder times for institutional forms of religion certainly have.

Bass offers helpful insights as to why those "harder times have come," and we will return to her in a moment. But first, let us examine the final of our evangelical phenomena, which marked the movement in the final half of the twentieth century. We address it last, though it is arguably the most telling. This is because while it may not have garnered the most headlines, this unique evangelical phenomenon may, however, be most iconic of the modern age in which evangelicalism, allied with its Enlightenment siblings, empiricism and rationality, reached its high-water mark. This final evangelical phenomenon was the widespread apologetics movement, cresting in the 1970s.

Christian Apologetics—The High-Water Mark of Evangelical Modernity

In 1947 Francis Schaeffer moved to Europe with his wife, Edith, to work with the Independent Board for Presbyterian Missions.[52] In the early 1950s, Schaeffer discovered he had a passion for philosophy and apologetics, and was especially drawn to the needs and concerns of the young. A trinity of his most foundational books, *Escape from Reason*, *The God Who Is There*, and *He Is There and He Is Not Silent*, were written and released as the late 60s slid into the early 70s.[53] Through the 1970s Schaeffer was lauded as an evangelical rock star. His book and film *How Should We Then Live?* took the Christian world by storm and in 1977, on the coattails of these productions, Schaeffer launched a twenty-two-city speaking tour.

Curiously, even after having lived such a public and productive life, Schaeffer is not easy to categorize. Was he an apologist? A philosopher? Or

50. Ibid., 174.
51. Ibid., 174.
52. White, *What Is Truth?*, 64.
53. Harper, "Francis A. Schaeffer," 130.

perhaps primarily an evangelist simply employing all the tools available to him?

James Emery White, president of Gordon-Conwell Theological Seminary, shares an insightful story underscoring the tension between Schaeffer's evangelistic and apologetic urges. In 1977, on the aforementioned national tour, Schaeffer spoke before a packed Anaheim Convention Center in southern California. At the conclusion of his talk, Schaeffer opened the floor to questions, and hearty souls could venture to microphones strategically positioned on the Convention Center floor. As White describes it, a young student queried the famous author with a question that began, "Since you are a presuppositionalist, rather than an evidentialist . . ." Schaeffer cut him off, replying, "I'm neither. I'm not an evidentialist or a presuppositionalist. You're trying to press me into the category of a theological apologist, which I'm really not. I'm not an academic, scholastic apologist. My interest is in evangelism."[54] What White doesn't report is that upon Schaeffer's retort, the Convention Center erupted in a thunder of rapturous applause. The student attempted a follow-up question but was unable, as his mic was immediately cut off. The student wasn't attempting to embarrass Schaeffer or derail the presentation, but, rather, was legitimately curious as to the structure of Schaeffer's apologetic system. I know, because I was that young student.

The irony, as I saw it that evening, was that if Schaeffer publicly eschewed the role of apologist for that of evangelist, what could have been his purpose in filling the Convention Center with the already converted? I left the Center that evening concluding that Schaeffer might have been annoyed at my query and perhaps elected to simply play to the crowd. Their quick applause seemed to indicate such. Kenneth Harper, a Schaeffer apologist and enthusiast, deals with the question posed that evening. He suggests that Schaeffer's strength rightly came from his "reticence to enter into the discussion between the different schools of apologetic methods," and concludes that even in his more philosophically comprehensive books Schaeffer's intent is not to present a finely crafted philosophical system, but "His purpose is rather evangelistic."[55] Finally, Harper emphasizes that "Schaeffer can only be understood as a prophet and an evangelist."[56] Perhaps, though if an evangelist, Schaffer was one quick to employ his ready arsenal

54. White, *What Is Truth?*, 71.

55. Harper, "Francis A. Schaeffer," 141.

56. Ibid., 140.

of rationalism, reason, and his confidence in undeniably catholic truths—the building blocks of a then-hegemonic modernity. But, as an apologist, Schaeffer was not alone, laboring alongside a cadre of fellow apologists who also thrived in that decade.

One such laborer was John Warwick Montgomery, a brilliant lecturer who released a flurry of apologetics books. Montgomery leaned heavily on historical arguments to support the faith. One of his books, the iconic title of which squarely affirms the author's posture and position, is unflinchingly entitled *Faith Founded on Fact: Essays in Evidential Apologetics*.

Another apologetics colaborer was the philosopher Richard L. Purtill. In his book *Reasons to Believe*, he cites human reason as trustworthy, load-bearing timber. As such, "reason must, of course," argues Purtill, "judge the credentials of any alleged revelation." And also, "if reason gives us no reason to suppose a given statement is a revelation from God, then we cannot believe it on those grounds . . . it is up to reason to test whether or not the alleged revelation is in fact a revelation from God."[57]

Another popular 1970s apologist was Paul Little. The popular Inter-Varsity Christian Fellowship worker authored *Know Why You Believe* in 1975. Little insists, "The gospel is always equated with truth. Truth is always the opposite of error."[58] Ultimately, Little flatly concludes, "Christianity is rational."[59]

Not even a quick trip through the apologetics legacy that was the 1970s would be complete without a mention of Josh McDowell. His standard apologetics "Bible," *Evidence That Demands a Verdict*, appeared in that decade and could be seen under the arms of armies of enthusiastic young believers of that era. Very early on in the latest updated edition of his standard, McDowell sets the tone for his work: "Christianity is a FACTual faith."[60] The touching irony of McDowell's apologetics books is the inclusion of his own salvation story, told against the backdrop of the deep humiliation and pain of his own father's alcoholism and his severe mistreatment of McDowell's mother. Perhaps McDowell's own coming to faith entailed evidences that did, indeed, demand a verdict. He doesn't say, but the touching sharing of his and even his father's ultimate coming to grace remind one less of a rational, jurisprudential exercise than it does a

57. Purtill, *Reasons to Believe*, 11.

58. Little, *Know Why*, 3.

59. Ibid., 6.

60. McDowell, *New Evidence*, xx.

gracious road-to-Damascus retelling. Evidence may be knowable, and even rightly demand a verdict, but even so, as McDowell's own journey to faith underscores, God's grace ever embodies what Rudolph Otto describes as the *mysterium tremendum*.

This quick survey of the Christian apologetics phenomenon of the 1970s underscores an important truth. It is that however postured on the philosophical playing field these tireless apologists may have been, as children of the Enlightenment, they all presupposed rock-ribbed tenets of modernity. Reason was regarded as a sure guide, the senses assumed to be reliable in the collection and marshalling of evidence, and pan-cultural universal systems could be logically built, expressed, trusted, and comprehended.

To summarize, then, evangelicalism at the close of the twentieth century was marked by five unique phenomena: 1) the charismatic movement, 2) the Jesus People revolution, 3) the church growth movement, 4) the rise of the Religious Right, and finally, 5) the rise and popularity of Christian apologetics. While each of these affected evangelicalism in its own unique ways, it was arguably the last of these—the apologetics of the 1970s—that served as the high-water mark of late-twentieth-century evangelical Christianity. This is because the apologetics of that era were as firmly seated upon parallel philosophical foundations as was Enlightenment modernity. Sensory observation was to be trusted, empiricism was the default, objectivity was assumed, and a universal (and obvious) rationality was the assumptive starting (and ending) point.

But any high-water mark contains within itself the irony of its own inevitable ebb. As quickly as it reaches its apex, the retreat begins. In a similar fashion, even as those of the apologetics movement were marshalling their rationalistic tools, developed and conveyed upon the seeming unassailable premises of the Enlightenment, the movement's retreat had already begun.

4

Evangelicalism: Ebbing?
or Simply Changing?

"In those days there was no king in Israel.
Everyone did what was right in his own eyes."

—Judges 21:25

ONCE, LOST DEEP IN the High Sierras, I found myself hiking up a narrow, high-walled canyon, affording just a thin ribbon of overhead blue. The weather was pleasant but, growing fatigued, I decided to sit for fifteen minutes to catch my breath. As I rested, I noticed that while superficially quiet and peaceful, the forest was alive in a cacophony of sound as the small animals darted about on the forest floor in a near-manic state. I concluded that they must sense a barometric pressure change that I could not detect. On this hunch, I donned my poncho and resumed hiking. Fifteen minutes later, the blue sky was now black and I was hammered by driving rain, thunder booming off the cliff sides. My hunch had been right, and watching the small animals had paid off. I concluded that while I might know *many* things, they knew *one* thing—that *nothing* was not happening and they had better seek shelter. And they were right.

In a similar sense, the evangelical world today is showing signs of frenetic activity in which its actors are showing that they too are acutely aware that *nothing is not happening*. Evangelicalism as a movement and evangelicals themselves are giving evidence of acting in response to great changes around them, and perhaps even *in* them.

Quantifying Nothing Not Happening

Perhaps one of the easiest means we have of measuring change within evangelicalism is to review the measures scholars such as James Davison Hunter has applied to the movement. In fact, the statistics Hunter reports show a steady decline in evangelical numbers, particularly in North America. While in 1900 41 percent of the population could be identified as theologically conservative, by 1980 that percentage had fallen over 20 percent to just 31.7 percent.[1]

In a more recently conducted Pew study, we see the percentages of 1980 degrading further still, with just 26.3 percent of Americans identifying as evangelicals.[2] At this point we might expect some Big Data gear heads to wickedly prognosticate that, given this trend, evangelicalism could be expected to completely disappear by the year . . . TBD. Demographic trends aside, there are others, thinking more theologically, who suggest that evangelicalism as classically conceived could completely disappear, even before evangelicals themselves grow extinct. More on this discussion below, but for now it is a worthy question to inquire as to where those bleeding away from the evangelical column are going. The Pew study addresses this question and concludes, "More than one-quarter of American adults (28%) have left the faith in which they were raised in favor of another religion—or no religion at all."[3] The study then finds that "the number of people who say they are unaffiliated with any particular faith today (16.1%) is more than double the number who were not affiliated with any particular religion as children."[4]

Diana Butler Bass and others describe this growing category of the religiously unaffiliated as "Nones," as in "None of the above." Bass points out that while in 1960 the self-identified "Nones" registered so slightly as to be immeasurable, just twelve years later the "Nones" had jumped from 0 percent to 5 percent of the population. This trend has continued, and by the year 2012, "depending on the survey used, some 16 to 20 percent of Americans are 'Nones,' making their numbers roughly equal to or slightly higher than the number of mainline Protestants."[5] In further analyses, David Kin-

1. Hunter, *Evangelicalism*, 5.
2. Pew Forum, "U.S. Religious Landscape Survey," 5.
3. Ibid., 5.
4. Ibid., 5.
5. Bass, *Christianity*, 46.

naman, president of the Barna Group, drills down further to explain of these "Nones" that the trend is "absolutely driven by younger people," and that millennials (those who demographers often identify as having been born from 1982 to 2004) "are twice as likely to be religiously unaffiliated."[6] When demographers that study birth rates of nations encounter negative trends such as this, we generally see great hand-wringing on their part, accompanied by warnings that the birth rates of the countries in question are so low as to fail to even meet replacement birth rates. In other words, flatly stated, such a nation, or religion, can only sustain negative replacement rates for a limited time until (statistically speaking, at least) it will ultimately disappear. Evangelical theologians and thinkers are generally not demographers, but these foreboding trends have not escaped them.

Looking more closely at these trends, Bass observes that "In 1985, 26 percent of young adults under twenty-nine claimed to be evangelicals; that number now (2012) hovers around 15 percent, while the number of 'Nones' under twenty-nine has risen from 12 percent to nearly 30 percent."[7] Given these data, it is no mystery as to where the young evangelical refugees are now setting up camp. Many of these youthful evangelical expats now consider themselves "Nones."

Learning to Define and Quantify Success

It was the 1980s, the decade of power. Power lunches and power ties. Coming from the advertising agency world, I had managed to finagle my way into my first legitimate executive marketing role. The company was a fast-lane mergers and acquisitions firm, swimming in a sea of roiling testosterone. I was the director of marketing, festooned in my own newly purchased three-piece suit. The founder and CEO was a formidable, tightly wound visionary from New York City who, if he ever relaxed, had never been witnessed doing so by anyone in the office.

My role was to manage our national lead generation campaign, which fueled the larger mergers and acquisitions machine. It is not an exaggeration to say that my performance came under the daily—or rather, hourly—scrutiny of our hard-driving CEO. As my performance directly affected the entire company, he was not about to assume anything. One morning, after I had been at the company a few weeks and had begun to

6. Fowler, "As minority," lines 14–16.

7. Bass, *Christianity*, 81.

produce measurable results, the CEO burst into my office and asked for the results of the day thus far. I gave him the numbers, in numbers. He looked at me, wordless, and then simply stated, "You're not telling me what I need to know." He exited, shutting the door behind him. This dance continued for several days. I gave him numbers; he exited, dissatisfied. Next, I tried percentages. And then even the delta over the previous day's results, again in raw numbers and also in percentages. Still the same response, "You're not telling me what I need to know," the door slamming behind him.

Finally, after about a week of mutual frustration, he entered my office and asked his usual question. This time, however, I presented my information not in raw numbers or percentages, but in *dollars*. He looked at me silently for a moment, pausing. "Finally. Now you're telling me what I need to know." With that, he allowed himself a slight smile, turned, and exited. This liberal arts major had just learned a valuable lesson. Two, actually. First, to successfully communicate with him, I needed to speak his language. This meant talking dollars, not raw numbers or percentages. Second, to succeed in that environment I needed to clearly understand how he defined and measured success.

The application here from the world of mergers and acquisitions to the world of religion is clear. If evangelicals, their world, and their movement are changing, an effective evaluation of these changes can only be made providing we have first established a clear definition of success. And of failure. If we are unable to clearly define success, we cannot meaningfully evaluate the effects of changes on and in the evangelical world. All we will know is what the animals on the forest floor know—that *nothing* is not happening. For instance, the above statistics, which underscore the steady and seeming decline of evangelicalism in North America, would seem to clearly chronicle evangelicalism's declining success rate or market share. But again, are these raw, statistical reports legitimate measures with which to evaluate the relative success of evangelicalism? No less a respected figure than Dallas Willard seems to be wrestling with the same question in his foreword to Dave Tomlinson's *The Post Evangelical*. Willard observes that evangelicalism has succeeded and . . . "achieved remarkable acceptance and prominence in recent decades . . ." but, even so, he muses wistfully, "We haven't figured out what the spiritual life is really like, inside and out." He continues by adding, "We haven't dealt successfully with the challenge of transforming our characters into routine Christlikeness."[8]

8. Tomlinson, *Post Evangelical*, 12.

Willard's candid musings could actually leave one nearly dumbstruck. If he is correct, and evangelicalism as a world-class religious movement has enjoyed "acceptance and prominence" across the past several decades, but failed to "figure out" the nature of the spiritual life—and likewise, may be failing to adequately pass this treasure on to its young—perhaps it should come as no surprise that an increasingly large number of young evangelicals are no longer evangelicals, but now "Nones." Such a shocking admission, especially coming from such a respected evangelical leader, could even have someone from another business—say, the mergers and acquisitions world—asking, "Well, if you're in the religion business but haven't 'figured out the nature of the spiritual life,' what business are you actually *in*? And, what have you been doing for the past seventy-five years?" But such a question would be cynical. Or would it? Consider the current Emergent "conversation," which is affecting nearly every quarter of evangelicalism. When one surveys the vast (and growing) body of Emergent work, it cannot be missed that the strands of the conversation are varied. Nonetheless, the theme of dissatisfaction with the status quo is consistent, and those in this movement should be regarded as making a fruitful contribution.

It might not be fair to attempt a one-to-one correlation between the Emergent movement as described by Peter Rollins, Dave Tomlinson, Phyllis Tickle, Brian McLaren et al., and the more statistically oriented George Barna. Even so, Barna's description of those exhibiting this growing dissatisfaction with the status quo churches is helpful. "They have no use for churches that play religious games, whether those games are worship services that drone on without the presence of God or ministry programs that bear no spiritual fruit."[9]

This expressed dissatisfaction on the part of the younger evangelicals with "the norm," and impatience with "religious games," is welcomed and might provide a hint as to a worthy answer to the above Willard-inspired question. "So, if evangelicalism hasn't been successfully figuring out the nature of the spiritual life," what *has* it been doing over these decades besides winning "acceptance and prominence?" While perhaps harsh, the question is not without merit. Indeed, the yearning for authenticity of spirituality, especially on the part of younger Emergent Christians, consistently wafts off nearly every syllable of their books, blogs, and posts. Kevin Corcoran of Calvin College explains this urge as a "turn away from Christianity as

9. Barna, *Revolution*, 15.

believing or *knowing* certain things and a turn toward Christianity as opening oneself up to a transformative *event*."[10]

While the diminishing evangelical body count might not be overly reassuring, perhaps numbers alone shouldn't be the sole measure of success. While cascading numbers likely underscore that in the evangelical world *nothing, indeed, is not happening*, it is still possible that naked statistics are inadequate to actually convey the true health of the movement. Again, Willard's insightful observation tips us off to the thought that, in matters religious, perhaps a measure capable of capturing the qualitative and not simply the quantitative is to be sought. In fact, might it not even be that as evangelical numbers have diminished, the spiritual health of the remaining faithful has strengthened and more than made up for the reduction in the ranks? Certainly there is precedent for this in the Scriptures themselves, as Gideon would attest. Likewise, might there be a silver lining in the dark cloud of the cascading numbers of youthful evangelical faithful across the recent decades? Some might, in the face of this trend, even suggest that a leaner, meaner, and more efficient evangelicalism could result from this culling of the herd. After all, wouldn't most put their wager on twenty highly-trained and lethal Navy Seals rather than even a small army of ambivalent conscripts? Most assuredly. But, of course, this illustration calls into question the relative "battle readiness" of the remaining evangelicals currently making up the approximate quarter of today's American population. Have these Americans self-identifying as evangelicals truly gotten meaner, or simply leaner?

If "battle readiness" can in any sense be equated to the successful living out of one's evangelical faith as a stranger in a strange land, what might this readiness look like? At this point, in terms of measurement, we are arguably moving from a quantitative to a more qualitative look. As we do so, it should be recognized that, especially as related to matters of the heart, one is faced with the challenge that such matters can be difficult to quantify. Slightly less difficult to measure, perhaps, are matters of attitudes and behaviors, which sociologists of religion have attempted to use as indices of underlying spiritual health.

10. McKnight et al., *Church in the Present*, 13.

Measuring Signs of Spiritual Life and Health

Justin Farrell of Notre Dame recently attempted this in his study "The Young and the Restless? The Liberalization of Young Evangelicals," conducted in 2011. Considering four central issues—young evangelicals' attitudes toward pornography, cohabitation, premarital sex, and abortion—Farrell found that on each issue excepting abortion younger evangelicals are significantly less inclined than older evangelicals to agree with the classical evangelical mores against pornography, cohabitation, and premarital sex. Specifically, Farrell discovered that younger evangelicals are 70 percent "more likely than older evangelicals to disagree with the statement that it is morally wrong to view pornography."[11] He also found that younger evangelicals are nearly two times "more likely to believe that it is a good idea to live together before marriage."[12] Likewise, concerning premarital sex, Farrell's study determined that younger evangelicals are 41 percent "more likely to disagree with the statement that premarital sex is wrong."[13] Finally, as indicated above, Farrell discovered that when abortion is considered, the younger evangelicals' attitudes "do not differ from older evangelicals.[14]

The reasons behind these generational differences are likely varied though. Farrell hypothesizes that "Older evangelicals tend to believe that God is the source of moral authority, and younger evangelicals believe that their own personal conscience is the true arbiter of right and wrong."[15] This hypothesis seems supported by the results of a national study conducted by Smith and Snell in 2009, in which the authors similarly concluded that emerging adults "are autonomous agents who have to deal with each other, yes, but do so entirely as self-directing choosers."[16] In the face of what their elders might regard as alarming trends, Farrell is quick to temper his findings by stressing, "This article only measures attitudes of young evangelicals, not the behaviors of young evangelicals."[17] Unfortunately, this sunny tempering might itself be tempered by the reminder from Proverbs, "For as he calculates in his soul, so is he" (Prov 23:7). Case in point: while Farrell

---

11. Farrell, "Young and the Restless?," 525.

12. Ibid., 526.

13. Ibid. 526.

14. Ibid. 526.

15. Ibid., 528.

16. Smith and Snell, *Souls*, 49.

17. Farrell, "Young and the Restless?," 529.

measured younger evangelical's *attitudes* toward pornography, in a 2011 dissertation Paul Chelsen reported on the actual Internet pornography usage of male students at evangelical Christian colleges. He found that "79.3 percent of male undergraduate students at evangelical colleges reported accessing Internet pornography at some point in the previous year with 61.1 percent reported accessing Internet pornography at least some amount of time each week."[18] In any case, clearly the jury is still out, awaiting the full fruition of the attitudes of young evangelicals into fixed behaviors. Farrell, for his part, summarizes the mindset of younger evangelicals by simply offering, "younger evangelicals are more liberal than older evangelicals."[19]

Evidences of the Evangelical Generational Divide

If one were to search for the reasons underlying the attitudes of the younger evangelicals, at least three would likely be good candidates. First is the challenge of living in an extremely liberal culture with maximized freedoms, with the temptations (or options) this presents. Some have suggested that, in the main, evangelicals have not met these challenges with great degrees of success. Noll, Plantinga, and Wells flatly assert, "Evangelicals have become remarkably worldly, accepting without debate, without question— often without notice—the assumptions, practices, and worldview of the larger American culture."[20] We might agree that these arguably distressing attitudinal changes on the part of the younger evangelicals are notable. We might then even commiserate with the assessment of Noll, Plantinga, and Wells in their dour observation. But this still begs the question, why? Why these dramatic attitudinal changes? And if Noll et al. are correct, why the evangelical acquiescence to the worldly "assumptions, practices, and worldview"?

Second, in addition to the challenge of living in a culture whose values are antithetical to what might be recognized as traditional evangelical mores, there is the matter of the contemporary family, Christian or not. In a recent study seeking to ascertain the reasons behind the Christian college enrollment boom of the past ten or so years, two central causes are cited. First, is the issue of the morally vacuous barbarism many parents see reigning in the contemporary public university, an environment many parents

18. Chelsen, "Examination," 106, 107.
19. Farrell, "Young and the Restless?", 517.
20. Noll et al., "Intellectual Failure," 497.

wish to avoid for their young. But the researchers also cite another factor. "For some harried parents, *en loco parentis* is attractive from their perspective, because divorces, careers and their own battles with drugs and alcohol have withered their capacity to parent."[21] In other words, Christian parents are depending upon the Christian colleges to adopt a significant role in the formation of their young evangelical offspring.

In addition to these factors—an aggressive culture whose values are arguably inimical to those of classical evangelicalism, along with the stresses on contemporary families today—there is yet another factor drawing the attention and study of an increasing number of researchers and thinkers. This is that of the evangelical churches themselves, which certainly should be expected to significantly contribute to the formation of all evangelicals, including the young. But at least one influential observer, in sizing up the performance of contemporary evangelical churches, offers a discouraging report card.

Barna Numbers the Troops

In *Revolution*, his search for and report on "vibrant faith beyond the walls of the sanctuary," George Barna enthusiastically reports on what he interprets as positive spiritual yearnings, especially in the youth. "Millions of devout followers of Jesus Christ are repudiating tepid systems and practices of the Christian faith and introducing a wholesale shift in how faith is understood, integrated, and influencing the world."[22] Barna calls these devout repudiators of tepid faith "Revolutionaries," and enthusiastically estimates their numbers as "well over twenty million strong," who "have no use for churches that play religious games, whether those games are worship services that drone on without the presence of God or ministry programs that bear no spiritual fruit."[23] He then delivers statistics on what he has found on the spiritual condition of the seventy-seven million Americans whom he identifies as churchgoing, born-again Christians:

- The biweekly attendance at worship services is, by believers' own admission, generally the only time they worship God.

21. "Why Christian Colleges Are Booming."
22. Barna, *Revolution*, 13.
23. Ibid., 15.

- Eight out of every ten believers do not feel they have entered into the presence of God, or experienced a connection with Him, during the worship services.

- Half of all believers say they do not feel they have entered into the presence of God or experienced a genuine connection with Him during the past year.

- Only 9 percent of all born-again adults have a biblical worldview—meaning that less than one out of every ten Christians age eighteen or older believes that absolute moral truth exists, believes that such truth is contained in the Bible.

- The other 91 percent of born-again adults possess a patchwork of theological views and rarely rely upon those perspectives to inform their daily decisions.[24]

These bleak findings are complemented by Barna's equally distressing synopses specifically related to the health of the evangelical churches themselves:

- A large majority of churched believers rely upon their church, rather than their families, to train their children to become spiritually mature.

- The likelihood of a married couple who are born-again churchgoers getting divorced is the same as couples who are not disciples of Jesus.

- Apart from church-based programs, the typical Christian family spends less than three hours per month in endeavors designed to jointly develop or apply their faith.[25]

In these observations, Barna's parallels those of Noll, Plantinga, and others cited above. But at this point, he offers a solution to these conditions, the radical ramifications of which will become more evident as we further survey the phenomenon of the "Emerging Church" (or "conversation") below. Says Barna: "The point here is simply to recognize that if we place all our hope in the local church, it is a misplaced hope."[26] Then, as if to soften the blow, he adds, "But the local church many have come to cherish—the services, offices, programs, buildings, ceremonies—is neither biblical, nor unbiblical. It is abiblical . . . We should keep in mind that what we call

24. Ibid., 31–33.
25. Ibid., 35.
26. Ibid., 37.

'church' is just one interpretation of how to develop and live a faith-centered life. We made it up."[27]

Could Barna be correct, not only in his dire assessment of the efficacy of the local church, but also in his comforting admonishment not to worry, since as regards the local evangelical church, we simply "made it up" anyway? The ancillary questions cited above also come to mind. First, how should we measure evangelical success? Second, if as a religious body we have reached the dizzying heights of Willard's "remarkable acceptance," but still lack an understanding of the spiritual life, and see a generation of young evangelicals whose spiritual formation is lacking, what business are we *in*, anyway? In what vineyard have we been toiling for the past decades? Fair questions, it would seem.

Church "Success" That Demands a Verdict

Two pastors who built a big, growing, exciting, and "successful" church, and lived to tell about it, are Kent Carlson and Mike Lueken. They tell the story of their conversion in their memoir, *Renovation of the Church*. Their conversion, that is, from what they call "the large entrepreneurial, attractional-model church,"[28] to one in which the definition and metrics of success themselves are refashioned and taught. While both had embraced the strategies and tactics of the seeker-friendly model, realizing dramatic church growth in the process, both crashed, unable and unwilling to pound the drum and lead the parade one step further. They concluded that "from a performance perspective, we had put together a first-rate product." As they continued to grow and excel in this "Disney formula," a friend, marveling at their success, commented, "You know, you don't even need God to do this."[29] Carlson and Lueken were sobered, but pressed on. They had trained their church members to be consumers, and as Carlson and Lueken recount, "the monster had now been created, and it demanded to be fed."[30] Superficially, no one could fault the two pastors. As they now recount, "The idea is that our communication of the unchanging gospel has to adapt to the ever-changing needs of our culture and audience. We had used this as a defense for the unconventional, innovative methods we employed to

27. Ibid., 37.
28. Carlson and Lueken, *Renovation*, 27.
29. Ibid., 24.
30. Ibid., 24.

communicate the gospel in our seeker days."[31] Despite their successes, they grew increasingly discouraged and exhausted, concluding that they had accomplished little more than birthing a congregation of spiritual consumers, grown fat and lazy on a continuous diet of quasi-spiritual junk food.

The two pastors slammed into their own inflection point when, finally, utterly exhausted and discouraged, they began searching for a new model, for a new definition of "church growth." In doing so, in part, they looked forward by looking back. They rediscovered and explored Christian spirituality as found in the writings of saints such as Teresa of Avila, Bernard of Clairvaux, and John of the Cross, augmented by those of Thomas Merton, Henri Nouwen, Richard Foster, and Eugene Peterson. The result was a dramatic reorientation of their concepts of both ministry and church growth. Indeed, "church growth" was transformed, for them, into growth of the church focused around the slow, intentional emphasis on the spiritual formation of their flock. And while they initially witnessed a significant exodus of parishioners, the two pastors persisted in their new understanding. Carlson and Lueken report that, for them, perhaps the toughest concept to abandon was that of the missional thrust being the raison d'etre of the local church, in which the congregants are fired up to go out and "make a difference."[32] As Carson and Lueken conclude the telling of their story, they suggest that in spite of its seeming success, "the church in North America is in serious trouble . . . we believe the patient is indeed desperately sick and needs to recover from a religious system that places a premium on outward success."[33]

Could it be possible that Carson and Lueken's personal church experience is a metaphor for that of the evangelical experience in North America today? In short, could it be that evangelicalism is exhausted, in part, from embracing and aspiring to a fraudulent metric of success? Even if this is not entirely true, it yet remains true that "nothing is not happening" and the animals on the forest floor are scurrying about seeking shelter—and the exits. Again, as shown above, a growing number of especially youthful evangelicals are voting with their feet and migrating from the evangelical column to that of "None of the above."

Again, since its inception fifty to sixty-plus years ago, evangelicalism in North America has been a growth industry. Viewed from a market

31. Ibid., 57.
32. Ibid., 108, 109.
33. Ibid., 15.

perspective, a product enjoys increasing market share so long as its "buyers" see it as a worthy solution to a perceived problem. Once a particular product is no longer seen as the best solution to the perceived problem, that product will suffer the erosion of its market share. In short, its "customers" migrate to other, more attractive products that promise better solutions to perceived problems. For decades, evangelicalism represented the best solution or "product" for a critical mass of North Americans of religious persuasion. This near monopoly, it seems, is rapidly eroding.

If this crass business/marketing evaluation of evangelicalism's current predicament is of any value and validity, it might also be legitimate and constructive to ask a related question from the inventory of business and marketing queries. Simply, if evangelicalism's origins can legitimately be placed at about the midpoint of the twentieth century, one might rightly ask, "If evangelicalism was the best answer for that time, what was *the question* of that time?" Asked another way, "If evangelicalism was the best solution (or answer) offered at that point, what was the problem (or question) at that point?" The benefit of asking these questions could be great with the resulting ramifications very constructive. For instance, if we were to discover that the original questions for which the genesis of evangelicalism was the best answer have changed, or are no longer even relevant, perhaps the answer itself—evangelicalism—is also nearing the end of its relevance. Or at least if the "solution" that is evangelicalism and its manner of spirituality and of "doing church" no longer solves today's "problem," perhaps it is time to seek out new, post-evangelical ways of living spiritually and of "doing church."

Could Barna be right in his assertion that the evangelical manner of church must change, and should change, especially insofar as we may have just "made it up" anyway? Is the survival of evangelicalism itself at risk as the demographic bulge that was the baby boomers loses its grip on the levers of social and cultural influence and power?

To wrestle constructively with these questions, it will help to go back in time to explore the modern context in which evangelicalism came of age—an age that changed radically, and whose changes would not leave evangelicalism untouched.

5

Ideas Have Consequences
Evangelicalism Collides with Postmodernity

AS WE HAVE ALREADY explored the paradigm of modernity, it is time now to turn our attention to the phenomenon of *post*modernity. This is critical, because the philosophical effects of postmodernity are not without substantial impact on a growing number of (especially) younger evangelicals, the net result of which is that a growing number of younger evangelicals are rejecting their fathers' evangelicalism—the evangelicalism, one might say, of the "A" versus the "Non-A."

Years ago, in the spring of 1972, I sat in the class of a professor I had studiously avoided for nearly two years. The highly regarded and duly beloved Dr. O was regarded by us mere undergraduates as possessing a near-godlike intellect. I had avoided his required apologetics class until the calendar afforded me no options. So on one beautiful spring afternoon, I sat as the professor launched into his thankless project of transforming us callow sophomores into fearless *defensors fide*.

The light of a young semester dancing in his eyes, Dr. O turned from us and chalked a giant "A" on its left side of the blackboard. Then, leaving an expanse, he added a sizable "Non-A" to the right. He turned and explained how the "A" could not, logically, also be the "Non-A." He was laying the groundwork for the logical law of non-contradiction, a foundational necessity for his apologetics. Once he had finished pointing out the crushing realities of the law, he paused and queried whether we had any questions. For us lowly students to question either Aristotle or, worse, Dr. O himself would have been like denying that the blackboard upon which he had written his "A" and "Non-A" was truly black! No one budged. Satisfied, he turned back to his blackboard. Actually, I *did* have a question. So I cleared my throat and tentatively raised my hand.

"Uh . . . Dr. O?"

"Yes," he replied, a flash of surprise across his face, wondering that any serious or sane human might question him or his logical law.

"I see your two points. I mean, the 'A' and the 'Non-A.' And I also see how they're held in tension, cannot touch and are always in contra-distinction. I get that. But," I continued, "both your points exist on a uni-dimensional plane. They're just sitting in one flat dimension. What if we imagined depth to the blackboard, along with multiple dimensions? If we can imagine such a world, where do your points sit then? Is it possible that your 'law of non-contradiction' is all of a sudden not such a given if all sorts of dimensions come into play?"

Actually, I didn't really know what I was talking about; it's just that his thesis seemed limited and unnecessarily unidimensional. What happened next I have never forgotten. Dr. O, in all his dignified scholarship, was stunned into silence. But only for a moment.

"Uh oh," I silently scolded myself, "why did you have to go and open your big mouth?"

Just then, he made a move like a Major League side-armed reliever, delivering a high and tight brushback fastball. He had wound up, his right hand still clutching the chalk, and delivered his "pitch," his body spinning until he had completed his delivery—his right arm in full extension aimed in my direction, his index finger extending toward my face. As he finished his spin and delivery, his feet firmly planted now and his body squaring to face me, he erupted in a near shout:

"You're a *mystic*!"

I didn't know him well enough to know whether he was trying to be funny, though, given his reputation, I made the quick assessment that this display—the "A"—could not, logically, also be humor—the "Non-A." (Perhaps Dr. O was right, after all!)

The quiet class didn't budge. The silence hung in the air for a long moment, his arm still outstretched. I didn't mean anything wrong by asking my question, or by saying what I said next. I really meant it.

"Thank you," I replied.

He didn't answer, nor expand on my newly ordained status as mystic. He simply turned, slowly, and resumed his lecture. I don't remember what grade I got in the class. It was certainly either an A or a non-A.

Recalling this episode, it has occurred to me that what Dr. O and I encountered together was no less than a clash of worldviews. Dr. O had been taught by scholars whose own intellectual roots first grabbed hold of the intellectual soil at the close of the nineteenth century! Considered this way, there was arguably close to a century's span between the respective philosophical assumptions held by Dr. O and myself.

The following year, my core requirements largely out of the way, I was finally free to take art classes, which I had looked forward to for some time. The brilliant art instructor teaching those courses once suggested that a milieu or culture advances like a spear flying through the air. Using this metaphor, he proposed that poets, artists, and writers formed the point of the cultural spear. If this thesis is at all true, then it could be very helpful to look to these actors for an understanding as to our culture's trajectory.

The Entrée of Postmodernity

Stanley Grenz provides an introduction to postmodern thought by first describing the backdrop of modernity, against which he then contrasts the makeup of the postmodern. Modernity, says Grenz, had its foundation in the Enlightenment, whose epistemological assumptions are uniquely identifiable. These included the assumptions that "knowledge is certain, objective and good."[1] Also, the Enlightenment-inspired moderns assumed that knowledge was accessible to the rational human mind and was consistently objective. Likewise, progress was assumed. Also assumed was the ideal of the autonomous, self-determining individual, who, as a self-determining subject, was seen to exist "outside any tradition or community."[2] "Postmodernism," however, asserts Grenz, "represents a rejection of the Enlightenment project and the foundational assumptions upon which it was built."[3] Taking Grenz's points here would thus lead us to conclude that, in contrast to the modern, for the postmodern mind, knowledge is *not* certain, *not* objective, and not necessarily good. Further, continued progress is doubted, suspect, and not assumed. Finally, rationality itself, for the postmoderns,

1. Grenz, *Primer*, 4.
2. Ibid., 4.
3. Ibid., 5.

is questioned. Indeed, for the postmodern the question becomes, "*Whose* rationality? *Whose* objectivity?" and even, "*Whose* reality?"

As Hicks asserts, postmodernism is "the supplanting of the Enlightenment with its roots in seventeenth-century English philosophy by the Counter-Enlightenment with its roots in the late eighteenth-century German philosophy. Kant is central to that story."[4] And Kant, in summary, suggests Hicks, effectively established that "the most important fact about reason is that it is clueless about reality."[5] Thus, concludes Hicks, while the empiricists of the Enlightenment believed that reality was what it was, independent of human consciousness,[6] for Kant, "real, noumenal reality is forever closed off to reason,"[7] and thus, external reality "drops almost totally out of the picture, and we are trapped inescapably in subjectivity."[8] Jean-Francois Lyotard, a pioneer of postmodern thought, echoes Kantian thinking when he cautions that "scientific knowledge does not represent the totality of knowledge; it has always existed in addition to, and in competition and conflict with another kind of knowledge, which I will call narrative in the interest of simplicity."[9]

In his classic, *Modern Times*, the historian Paul Johnson suggests that the hard-edged and solidly modern philosophical construct began to teeter in the 1920s when Albert Einstein's hypotheses of relativity began to find wide circulation. For the "man on the street," reports Johnson, "relativity became confused with relativism," and the "belief began to circulate, for the first time at a popular level, that there were no longer any absolutes; of time and space, of good and evil, of knowledge, above all of value."[10] In a manner of speaking, $E=MC^2$ was reduced to the glib, "Well, everything's relative." Ideas do, indeed, have consequences.

Similarly, most people "on the street" or in the mall today would likely offer a quizzical stare if asked to identify the persons, work, or ideas of Lyotard, Derrida, Rorty, Fish, or even Michael Foucault—leading lights of postmodern thought. Even so, not unlike Johnson's everyman, above, the young mall shopper who fails to identify even one of these thinkers would,

4. Hicks, *Explaining Postmodernism*, 43.

5. Ibid., 29.

6. Ibid., 33.

7. Ibid., 28.

8. Ibid., 41.

9. Lyotard, *Postmodern Condition*, 7.

10. Johnson, *Modern Times*, 5

nonetheless, likely be quick to assert, "Who's to say what's right or wrong?" and, "Like, if that's what's true for *you*, fine, but it's not what's true for *me*." Again, as Johnson summarized, Einstein's *relativity* was widely popularized as *relativism*. Similarly, as we are exiting modernity with its philosophical fixedness, we are entering a brave new world and mind in which, in its popular application, things, concepts, and truths are no longer fixed or even solid.

Middleton and Walsh describe one effect of this change by quoting the philosopher Albert Borgmann, who suggests, "An epoch approaches its end when its fundamental conviction begins to weaken and no longer inspires enthusiasm among its advocates."[11] Perhaps we might conclude that an epoch has certainly reached its end when the children of its fiercest followers hardly even compute with the philosophical assumptions of their elders. This may also explain how it is that today's younger evangelicals no longer buy into or even clearly comprehend some of the bedrock assumptions of their (still *modern*) evangelical elders.

Postmodernity may be well described as a thought system, or at least thought exercise, that has rejected "the notion of an independently existing reality, (and which) denies that reason or any other method is a means of acquiring objective knowledge of that reality."[12]

Political scientist Walter Truett Anderson offers a humorous illustration of three baseball umpires to illustrate three competing epistemological positions. The three umpires, writes Anderson, "are sitting around over a beer, and one says, 'There's balls and there's strikes, and I call 'em the way they are.' Another says, 'There's balls and there's strikes, and I call 'em the way I see 'em.' The third says, 'There's balls and there's strikes, and they ain't nothin' until I call 'em.'" This third umpire, asserts Truett, "is a postmodern radical."[13]

As we remember, Kant's contribution to Western thought was, in part, his paradigm-shifting assertion that we do not experience the actual stuff of reality, but rather that our minds create a reality through our encounter and ordering of the phenomena around us. Hence, Hicks concludes that while some earlier thinkers may have been nascent skeptics, they still "continued to conceive of truth as correspondence to reality. Kant went a

---

11. Middleton and Walsh, *Truth Is Stranger*, 11.

12. Hicks, *Explaining Postmodernism*, 6.

13. Anderson, *Reality*, 75.

step further and redefined truth on subjective grounds."[14] It is for this contribution, Truett suggests, that Kant is credited by some "for opening the door to postmodern thought."[15] Grenz amplifies this philosophical shift by explaining that "The loss of the modern worldview marks the end of the objective world of the Enlightenment project," and that in this loss, "the postmodern era has abandoned the notion of the object world, and moved from an objectivist to a constructionist outlook."[16]

While Grenz has correctly drawn our attention to postmodernity's serving as the fulcrum for the potential abandonment of a belief in an objective world, others, such as the scholar Allucuere Rosanne Stone, were early adopters of such possibilities. In her intriguing *The War of Desire and Technology at the Close of the Mechanical Age*, Stone studies the Internet and the possibilities it presents people for the creation of a second or even multiple identities. Stone neatly follows the logic of her exploration and concludes that the origin of the concept of one's "true identity" (or of even having one) "seems to have been contemporaneous with the Enlightenment, the same cultural moment that gave birth to what we like to call the sovereign self."[17] For Stone, we may in fact naturally possess no "true identity," and as a self-proclaimed transgendered person, she (he?) explains that "essentialists believe that sex and gender are the same thing . . . and usually believe there are only two genders; these are present at birth." She counters this view, claiming that "social constructionists believe that both sex and gender arise in social interaction and have no existence independent of social interaction; i.e., they are not grounded in 'nature,' the meaning of which itself is socially determined."[18] For the postmodern Stone, even identity as basic as one's gender is not a given, but rather a social construct.

The Notion of "Self," the "Spear's Tip" and the Social Construction of a New Reality

In her reference to social constructionists, Stone is not without precedent. The prolific sociologist Peter Berger wrote early on the concept of the social construction of reality. In his book of the same name, Berger anticipates

14. Hicks, *Explaining Postmodernism*, 41.

15. Anderson, *Reality*, 60.

16. Grenz, *Primer*, 40.

17. Stone, *War of Desire*, 75.

18. Stone, "Transgender."

Stone by hypothesizing, "The formation of the self, then, must also be understood in relation to both the ongoing organismic development and the social process in which the natural and the human environment are mediated through the significant others."[19] Likewise, Theodore Roszak, the history professor, and for many, the herald of the spirit of the 60s, explains that we "learn" or construct our worldview not only from the other actors on the stage with us, but also absorb it from the *zeitgeist* of our environment.

Recalling my art teacher's suggestion that the poets, writers, and artists on the "spear's tip" can alert us as to the coming twists, turns, and directions in culture, it is to this trio that we will now look in an effort to further explore postmodernity's origins.

In popular culture, "everybody knows" that the 1950s were sleepy, placid, and utterly boring. Corporatism, conservatism, and rationalism had won the day, and the culture of management was in the ascendancy. And yet, despite the seeming hegemony enjoyed by the empirically modern, there was a stirring beneath the pacific waters of the mainstream American culture of the mid-twentieth century.

Allen Ginsberg, the beat poet, best known for his iconic *Howl*, performed the first public reading of his signature poem at Six Gallery in San Francisco in 1955. Poetically chronicling what he regarded as the madness of an increasingly rigid and conformist society, Ginsberg's howls echoed through the ranks of the nascent Beat culture, heralding the ever so slight shifting of the modernist earth beneath their feet. Roszak celebrates *Howl* and its "remarkable anticipation of the Zen principle of the illuminated commonplace."[20]

The reading itself, celebrated as the genesis of the Beat Generation, was chronicled in a fictionalized account in *Dharma Bums*, written by Jack Kerouac, who gave the Beat Generation its name along with his own Beat chronicles, *On the Road* and *Dharma Bums*. Roszak weighed in on Kerouac and his *Dharma Bums*, astutely pointing out that the book was the "first handy compendium of all the Zen catch phrases that have since become more familiar to our youth than any Christian catechism."[21] In this bit of possible hyperbole, Roszak successfully underscores that for America's youth the traditional religious paradigm was, even then, teetering.

19. Berger and Luckmann, *Social Construction*, 50.

20. Roszak, *Making*, 131.

21. Ibid., 131.

Part of Zen's draw, notes Roszak, was both its assumption of paradox and value of silence. "Those who know do not speak; those who speak do not know," chants Roszak, contrasting Zen's commitment to a paradoxical and "wise silence, which contrasts so strongly with the preachiness of Christianity."[22] Roszak thus underscores that the Beat movement held the seeds and essence of a nascent spiritual shift that not only affected the cultural, but also the religious, or spiritual, *zeitgeist*.

This Beat unsettledness with the norm was echoed by the release of the *Doors of Perception*, written by the Englishman Aldous Huxley, who experimented with mescaline in his drug-aided efforts to pry open the doors of perception.

But in his drug-induced exploration of spiritual experience, Huxley was not alone. He was, in fact, positioned at the nexus of a nascent, though soon to be burgeoning, experimentation with what came to be known as psychedelics.

In the fall of 1960, the Harvard professor Timothy Leary was a single father raising two children alone, following the suicide of his wife, Marianne. While on summer vacation in Mexico, Leary was introduced to an old Mexican woman—a shaman—who would change his world forever. This *vieja* was a witch who collected and shared her magic mushrooms with the Harvard professor. Leary consumed the witch's mushrooms and fell into a three-hour-long altered state of consciousness, which he would later describe as an experience of seeing everything around him "quivering with life, even inanimate objects." Indeed, the experience that afternoon "shattered the foundation of his philosophy of life and his view of himself. He became convinced, on the basis of his mushroom trip, that what we call 'reality' was just a social fabrication. He would later call his trip 'the deepest religious experience of my life.'"[23]

Leary returned to Harvard and immediately organized what he called the Harvard Psilocybin Project. The project's goal was to introduce the use of the drug to colleagues and graduate students, and soon a collection of personalities who would ultimately become recognized as counterculture icons, gathered around Leary in his rambling old home. There was Andrew Weil, who, though then just a freshman, would ultimately come to be regarded by many as the father of the health and wholeness movement. Also in the circle of exploring associates was the Englishman Aldous Huxley, on

22. Ibid., 134.

23. Lattin, *Harvard Psychedelic*, 40–41.

loan to MIT as a guest lecturer. Richard Alpert, a Harvard psychology professor who would undergo a spiritual transformation, and ultimately travel to India to return rebranded as Ram Dass, also found himself in Leary's home. Rounding out the visitors to Leary's home were both Alan Watts and Allen Ginsberg.

The Beats and the Construction of a New Spiritual Reality

Given this nexus of drug use and the exploration of alternative spiritualities, it's no surprise that a strong spiritual theme runs through the Beat movement. Alan Watts, himself a bit player in Kerouac's *Dharma Bums*, began as an Episcopal priest, was driven from his pulpit by personal scandal, and made his own exodus from Western Christianity toward tantric belief. As he protested in his *The Book*, "Who wants to be stuck in church, wearing a surplice, and singing, 'Alleluia?' forever?"[24] Certainly not Watts himself, especially when he discovered that

> The "Ultimate Ground of Being" is Paul Tillich's decontaminated term for "God," . . . But the secret which my story slips over to the child is that the Ultimate Ground of Being is *you*. Not, of course, the everyday you which the Ground is assuming, or "pretending" to be, but that inmost Self which escapes inspection because it's always the inspector. This, then, is the taboo of taboos; you're IT![25]

Watts builds his case for the embrace of what he considers the ultimate taboo—the recognition that the individual self is, in fact, the ultimate "IT." For Watts, radical individuality is an illusion, and it is this "hallucination of separateness (which) prevents one from seeing that to cherish the ego is to cherish misery."[26] Indeed, suggests Watts, this is a misery that necessarily follows when one fails to grasp that separate egos are but an illusion and instead recognize that "every individual is a unique manifestation of the whole."[27] Furthermore, suggests Watts, this slavery to the illusion of radical individualism necessarily condemns modern humanity to live as

24. Watts, *Book*, 37.
25. Ibid., 18.
26. Ibid., 18.
27. Ibid., 79.

misguided conquistadors who consider the principal task of life "to get one-up on the universe and to conquer nature."[28]

To further make his point, Watts explored an ironic apex of the modern as embodied in theoretical physics. Citing the highly influential physicist David Bohm, who himself cast a disparaging glance toward the creaking Cartesian model, Watts quotes from Bohm's *Quantum Theory*, ". . . the world cannot be analyzed correctly into distinct parts; instead, it must be regarded as an indivisible unit in which separate parts appear as valid approximations only in the classical (i.e., Newtonian) limit . . ."[29] Watts was prescient in his early appeal to quantum physics to buttress his argument for a transcendence of the modern worldview, and bend the trajectory back toward the premodern.

Literary Canaries in the Cultural Coal Mine

In our effort to understand the shifting *zeitgeist* of North America, we would do well to review two additional cultural canaries in the coalmine before leaving our exploration of the spear's tip.

Carlos Castaneda, a Peruvian-American UCLA graduate student in anthropology, burst onto the scene with the publishing of his first book, *The Teachings of Don Juan: A Yaqui Way of Knowledge*. In the book, Castaneda recounts his spiritual tutelage at the feet of a spiritual sorcerer of the Yaqui tribe. Offered by Castaneda as an exercise (and perhaps allegory) in the understanding of reality, his experiences with don Juan strip away Castaneda's assumed, Western, rational construct of reality. Aided by the sorcerer's tools of peyote and magic mushrooms, don Juan bends and then breaks forever Castaneda's concept of physical and even spiritual reality. Castaneda, at his teacher's beckoning, begins the process of exiting the modern, rational, and rigid world. The zenith of Castaneda's discipleship to his Yaqui spiritual guide is reached when Castaneda, aided by his teacher's magic "devil weed," experiences flight. Or, at least, when he suspects he *may* have flown. In a humorous retelling of his flight, Castaneda queries his teacher and struggles with his own doubts of the experience.

"Did I really fly, don Juan . . . I mean did my body fly? Did I take off like a bird?"

28. Ibid., 80.
29. Ibid., 106.

The incredulous teacher, puzzled by his disciple's questions, replies, "You always ask me questions I cannot answer. You flew . . . that is all I can tell you. What you want to know makes no sense. Birds fly like birds and a man who has taken the devil's weed flies as such."

Still unsatisfied, Castaneda presses on. "As birds do?"

"No," instructs the teacher, a man "flies as a man who has taken the weed."

Castaneda, yet hemmed in by the guardrails of his own Western thought, presses again, for further clarification. "Then I didn't really fly, don Juan. I flew in imagination, in my mind alone. Where was my body?"

His teacher replies with a cutting retort. "In the bushes . . . the trouble with you is that you understand things in only one way. You don't think a man flies; and yet a *brujo* can move a thousand miles in one second to see what is going on . . . so does he or doesn't he fly?"

Still unconvinced, Castaneda counters: "You see, don Juan, you and I are differently oriented. Suppose, for the sake of argument, one of my fellow students had been here with me when I took the devil's weed. Would he have been able to see me flying?"

"There you go again with your questions about what would happen if . . . It is useless to talk that way."

His Western, "A"-versus-"non-A" paradigm still nagging, Castaneda tries one last time. "Let's put it another way, don Juan. What I meant to say is that if I had tied myself to a rock with a heavy chain I would have flown just the same, because my body had nothing to do with my flying."

To this question, Castaneda reports that don Juan "looked at me incredulously," answering, "If you tie yourself to a rock . . . I'm afraid you will have to fly holding the rock with its heavy chain."[30]

Whether or not Castaneda actually flew, rock or no rock, or whether Don Juan ever really existed, the power of the tale lies not in its historicity or lack thereof; instead, the import of a book like Castaneda's lay in the widespread embrace of the truths it purported to tell. Central to these was the breaking down and spurning of the body/mind dualism, itself a hallmark of modernity, as we have already seen. For an entire generation of 60s and 70s youths to embrace tales such as Castaneda's, and not blink at the prospect of actually soaring through the galaxy in flight, while one's body might yet be lying "in the bushes," could mean only one thing: the Dr. Os of the world were on the run. And even if their elders were yet unaware of the

30. Castaneda, *Teachings*, 129–30.

shaking of the foundations beneath their feet, the youth had already begun to leave the room. And the pews.

Indeed, while the Dr. Os were yet holding forth for unassailable truths of objective modernity, their students were groping, largely by feel, into alternative dimensions where the "As" and the "non–As" might no longer be conflicting, but rather complementary and perhaps even singular.

Of a differing genre than Castaneda's writings, though arguably of similar mind, the writings of Herman Hesse also found wide currency among the 60s youths, straddling, as they were, the growing chasm between the two ages, modern and post-.

Hesse, the German-born poet and novelist, wrote prolifically and was widely read by American youths coming of age in the 60s and 70s. Two Hesse titles stand out on account of their poignant dealing with his central concerns, these being, *journey, irony, paradox, unity,* and *spiritual enlightenment.*

In perhaps his best-known work, *Siddhartha,* Hesse tells the tale of a seeker who sets off on a journey to find himself, and in doing so achieves spiritual enlightenment. Siddhartha, the protagonist, ultimately embraces the irony of recognizing, "The people of the world were the equals of the sages in all else, were often far superior to them, just as animals are often superior to human beings . . ."[31] But Siddhartha's enlightenment doesn't stop here. As Hesse explains.

> There slowly bloomed and ripened in Siddhartha the realization and knowledge of what wisdom, the object of his long quest, really was. It was nothing more than a readiness of the soul, a mysterious knack: the ability at every moment in the midst of life to think the thought of unity, to feel and breathe unity.[32]

These familiar Hesse themes of quest, journey, irony, paradox, unity, and spiritual enlightenment are echoed dramatically in his short novella, *The Journey to the East.* This is a story of a mysterious and secretive sect and its pilgrimage to visit a revered and enlightened holy man. Hesse recounts the seemingly directionless journey in search of wisdom, describing the various characters along the way. One such character is a respected, though humble and lowly caravan laborer. Ultimately and ironically, the protagonist realizes his quest when he finally recognizes that the revered,

31. Hesse, *Siddhartha,* 128.
32. Ibid., 128–29.

enlightened, and holy man has been with the caravan all along, in the person of the meek, humble, and overlooked porter. Again, we can see in both these Hesse novels the willingness and even enthusiasm to dispense with recognized authority, embracing instead the overlooked, the humble, and the exotic as the ultimate source of authoritative wisdom.

Against this changing backdrop, the sociologist Peter Berger insightfully observed, "In the American religious-secular continuum of values, Christianity appears embedded in taken-for-granted reality. It does not stand out from the rest of culture, at least not in its middle-class Protestant forms."[33]

It would seem these poets and writers, along with the sociologists of religion of their era, were using different language, though agreeing on the message: a spiritual awakening was afoot and the traditional religion of Christianity, tied as it was to the "take it for granted" reality of Western middle-class American values, was on its heels. Indeed, the enlightenment of America's youth in the 60s and 70s was neatly summed up, again, by Theodore Roszak:

> For all its frequently mindless vulgarity, for all its tendency to get lost amid the exotic clutter, there is a powerful and important force at work in this wholesale willingness of the young to scrap our culture's entrenched prejudice against myth, religion, and ritual. The life of Reason (with a capital R) has all too obviously failed to bring us the agenda of civilized improvements the Voltaires and Condorcets once foresaw.[34]

Postmodernity and Straight vs. Stoned Thinking

In the fall of 1972 Andrew Weil wrote *The Natural Mind*, in which he argued for the recognition and embrace of what he suggested was a new way of thinking about thinking. He explained that the ordinary way of thinking, with which we are all familiar, was giving way to a superior mode of cognition.

The standard way of thinking Weil described as *straight thinking*, while he called this new mode of thought *stoned thinking*. Echoing the earlier Beat poets, Weil proposed that the standard mode of thought was

33. Berger, *Noise*, 116.
34. Roszak, *Making*, 145–46.

largely a result of ego-centered consciousness. This yielded, according to Weil, the static exercise of *straight thinking*, which he identified with five unique characteristics:

1. A tendency to know things through the intellect rather than through some other faculty of the mind. *(Here Weil explained his belief that the intellect, while important, is but a sole component of the mind. Thus, when one is operating exclusively on this level, one may be seduced into believing that he or she actually knows something due to their understanding it intellectually.)*

2. The tendency to be attached to the senses and through them to external reality. *(This attachment, according to Weil, results in our inability to free ourselves from, or step outside the continuous onslaught of the unending flow of scattered sensory phenomena. A freeing, according to Weil, is needed if we are to encounter a reality beyond the simple flow of sensory stimuli. To achieve this, suggested Weil, necessitates engaging in an altered state of consciousness.)*

3. A tendency to pay attention to outward forms rather than to inner contents and thus to lapse into materialism. *(By materialism, Weil was not thinking of acquisitiveness, but rather, the seduction of believing that reality does not transcend the material.)*

4. A tendency to perceive differences rather than similarities among phenomena. *(Here Weil underscores the importance of this tendency in Western science, and describes the ultimate distinction made by the straight intellect as that between the self and the not-self.)*

5. A tendency toward negative thinking.[35]

Weil sums up his description of *straight* thinking by suggesting "Straight thinking is straight in the way an interstate highway is straight in that it does not follow the natural contours of reality."[36]

In contrast, Weil describes what he calls *stoned thinking*, and lists as its tenets:

1. A reliance on intuition as well as intellection. *(Weil associated intuition with the unconscious mind, and while he made it clear that he*

---

35. Weil, *Natural Mind*, 119–34.
36. Ibid., 57.

did not reject intellection, there yet exists a source of direct information about reality that is available to us.)

2. An acceptance of the ambivalent nature of things. *(By this, Weil meant that in his view reality largely manifests itself in pairs of [seeming] opposites, an understanding embraced, according to Weil, by both adherents of Eastern religions and modern physicists.)*

3. The experience of infinity in its positive aspect.[37]

In 1967, the sociologist Thomas Luckmann wrote *The Invisible Religion*, in which he lobbied for a more expansive understanding of religion.

> Any ideological and social construction of reality can be labeled religion, if by its making humans show their transcendence over their purely biological nature. Science as a world system is thus as much religion as Catholicism. By this reckoning all societies however secular have a covert religion, and the more widely accepted such a religion is the more it is taken for granted, and so the more it is invisible.[38]

It was this unseen paradigm of thought in Western modernity that Luckmann describes, and Weil labels, as *straight thinking*. The social observer Ellwood concludes of Luckmann's 1967 book, "The book may be considered important as a 1967 publication because of the way it pried open a cognitive space for postmodern criticism of modernist universal truth systems like science."[39]

Physicists and the New (Construction of) Reality

If Luckmann's thesis is correct, and the philosophical construct of the modern mind may be equated to a belief system no less pervasive than an accepted scientific paradigm, then it may be accurate to suggest that in the turbulent era we have been describing, America was changing both its religion and its science. Indeed, as we have seen hinted above, it was the scientists—the physicists, to be exact—who were increasingly beginning to

37. Ibid., 149–56.
38. Ellwood, *60s*, 227.
39. Ibid., 227.

THEOSIS

posit a very anti-materialistic and paradigm-shifting view of nature, and of reality itself.

As we have already seen, the Newtonian worldview came onto the scene and posited a regular universe that was measurable, knowable, predictable, and reasonable. According to this new paradigm, the universe made sense, with or without God. Employing this new worldview allowed for major steps forward in science and technology, justifiably yielding a strong faith in the idea of the inevitably of progress. Such was the new modern physics, which arguably saw its zenith as physicists in the 1940s raced to understand, exploit, and ultimately achieve mastery of the atom.

But had they? Indeed, even as Japan still lay in flattened, smoldering ruins the physicists were having second thoughts. A growing number had already begun to speculate that there were mysterious subatomic, or quantum, worlds that behaved in curious and decidedly non-Newtonian ways.

While quantum theories are complex, with many moving parts still in the theoretical stage, former Special Forces soldier and science writer Gary Zukav attempts to explain quantum theory on a popular level:

> The mind-expanding discovery of quantum mechanics is that Newtonian Physics does not apply to subatomic phenomena. In the subatomic realm, we cannot know both the position and the momentum of a particle with absolute precision. We can know both, approximately, but the more we know about one, the less we know about the other . . . the two data which must be included in a Newtonian calculation, position and momentum, cannot both be known with precision. *We must choose*, by the selection of our experiment, which one we want to measure most accurately.[40]

The implications of this proposition are arresting because they hint that our observation, or at least conception, of quanta is dynamic and our perception or at least calculation of position on this level affects our ability to calculate momentum or velocity, and vice versa. Even more disturbing, perhaps, is the implication, suggested by some quantum physicists, that in some sense we may, in fact, be creating or affecting certain quantum properties by the very act of measurement. As the Princeton physicist John Wheeler expressed it,

> May the universe in some strange sense be "brought into being" by the participation of those who participate? . . . The vital act is the act of participation. "Participator" is the incontrovertible new

40. Zukav, *Dancing*, 53.

concept given by quantum mechanics. It strikes down the term "observer" of classical theory, the man who stands safely behind the thick glass wall and watches what goes on without taking part. It can't be done, Quantum mechanics says.[41]

At this point, comments Zukav, "the languages of eastern mystics and western physicists are becoming very similar."[42]

In another popular presentation of quantum mechanics and its possible ramifications, Margaret J. Wheatley describes the weak underbelly of the seemingly triumphant Newtonian model. This machine-like universe, which humanity had thought it had discovered and mastered, turned out to be a rather cold and even inhospitable home. In contrast, the strange, exotic quantum world was increasingly looking like a world into which we ourselves were knit, and in which "There are no either/ors." In addition, "There is no need to decide between two things, pretending they are separate. What is critical is the relationship created between two or more elements."[43] Or, borrowing language from Dr. O, perhaps this new vision is at least somewhat built on the eclipse of the model of the "A" versus the "non-A"?

As Zukav explains, at the base of quantum mechanics lies the concept of *complementarity*. The physicist Niels Bohr suggested the term to explain the curious phenomenon physicists observed when conducting experiments with light in which light could be observed both as a particle and also as a wave. In other words, light was not *either* a wave *or* a particle, but both/and, depending upon the nature of the experiment/observation. Seemingly, at the quantum level, mutual exclusivity—at least as regards the composition of light—is not necessary and cannot be assumed. Even more intriguing, suggests Zukav, is that there are no fixed properties of light. "They are properties of our *interaction* with light . . . The new physics tells us that an observer cannot observe without altering what he sees. Observer and observed are interrelated in a real and fundamental sense."[44]

Perhaps Zukav overstates the case here. Perhaps light exists whether or not humans or other beings exist to dance together in an affirmation of existence. Even so, and in any case, if the physicists are correct, the

41. Ibid., 54.

42. Ibid., 54.

43. Wheatley, *Leadership*, 35–36.

44. Zukav, *Dancing*, 115.

subatomic world they are exploring is not their fathers' universe. Or our fathers' consciousness or construct of reality.

David Bohm, the American physicist, proposes in his book *On Creativity* that, according to recent discoveries in physics,

> when one comes down to the atomic and subatomic level of size, the observing instrument is even in principle inseparable from what is to be observed. One may compare this situation to a psychological observation, which can likewise "disturb" the people being studied, and thus take part in the process that one wants to learn about, as well as "create" and shape some of the very phenomena that can be observed.[45]

But Bohm doesn't stop there. He pursues his line of logic to suggest that even science does not merely create theories that can be understood as reflections of nature. Instead, suggests Bohm, as observers we are incessantly building paradigms, which symbolize our *relationships* with nature. These paradigms, according to Bohm, are not actual nature or reality, but rather relationships, and should be held lightly. We should be ready, according to Bohm, to forfeit them for new paradigms that prove themselves more "true," based upon their greater degree of harmony, order, "elegance," unified totality, and even, says Bohm, beauty.[46] Scientific theories judged true by degrees of harmony? Order? Elegance and beauty? Certainly Bohm, standing on Newton's shoulders, has nonetheless left the exclusively measurable, mechanical, and predictable world of the Englishman far behind. Finally, citing Bohm, Wheatley suggests, "at a level we can't discern, there is an unbroken wholeness."[47]

But even so, for the paradigmatic reality of an entire *zeitgeist* to shift on a mass-merchandised level, much more than esoteric mathematical theories and even poetry had to be in play. And it was. Because at this point, given the increasingly singular and instantly communicating culture of the Western world, the youth of that world had their memorable mantra, and happily rhapsodized unhesitatingly along in unison about walruses and about being one, both with each other and also with the whole.

If this evolution from a hegemonic modernity into the embrace of a new quantum paradigm changed everything about how we understand the physical universe, it did not leave religion, or perhaps more accurately,

45. Bohm, *On Creativity*, 41.
46. Ibid., 42.
47. Wheatley, *Leadership*, 43.

spirituality, untouched. Indeed, for many, the confluence of these various social and scientific phenomena could mean only one thing: spiritually speaking, it was the dawning of a new age.

The Dawning of the New Age (of Aquarius)

Even if what would come to be regarded as "New Age" spirituality was, in the 1960s, still a small cloud the size of a person's hand, it was a cloud the prescient Theodore Roszak saw forming even before that storied decade had expired.

> This, so I have argued, is the primary project of our counter culture: to proclaim a new heaven and a new earth so vast, so marvelous that the inordinate claims of technical expertise must of necessity withdraw in the presence of such splendor to a subordinate and marginal status in the lives of men.[48]

Roszak elaborates, calling for open-mindedness toward the shamans of a past era, who had seemingly been stripped of their legitimacy by modernity's rationalism and scientism. In fact, Roszak suggests that being truly "civilized" should mean embracing a "willingness to consider as instructive examples all the human possibilities that lie within our intellectual horizon, including those that conventional wisdom tells us are hopelessly obsolescent."[49]

If Roszak was the prophet of the New Age, Marilyn Ferguson is arguably its chronicler. Ferguson's genius was to recognize the confluence of thought represented by these varied personalities from multiple disciplines and roll it all up into her 1980 release, *The Aquarian Conspiracy*. Ferguson explained that by "conspiracy" she did not mean a secretive plot planned and executed from hidden or obscure back rooms. Instead, she perceived a conspiracy in the classic sense of the "breathing together" of various and disparate forces into a mighty confluence. Ferguson explains:

> Something remarkable is underway. It is moving with almost dizzying speed, but it has no name and eludes description . . . the indefinable force is an idea whose time has come, and it is robust enough now to be named . . . after a dark, violent age, the Piscean,

48. Roszak, *Making*, 240.
49. Ibid., 242.

we are entering a millennium of love and light . . . a different age seems to be upon us.[50]

For those seeking to understand what she described as this new and "emergent culture," "Logic alone," she warned, echoing Weil, "is a poor prophet. Intuition is necessary, to complete this picture."[51] Indeed, for Ferguson, it was a non-rational or at least a-rational and non-linear mode of thought which was necessary to usher one into the desired state of, as she described it, "awareness of awareness."[52]

For her part, Ferguson foresaw this New Age transformation taking place universally, and dramatically altering a multiplicity of fields such as music, art, economics, technology, and politics. Concluding her study, she notes that modern humanity's appetites have left them gorged on materialism and yearning for spiritual substance. She cites Zbigniew Brzezinski, a Carter cabinet member, who gave voice to an "increasing yearning for something spiritual" in the Western world,[53] and points out that Brzezinski concluded that "traditional religion" has failed to deliver this desired spirituality"[54]—a conclusion with which Ferguson heartily agreed.

If an outbreak of New Age, a-rational spirituality seems incongruous with Americans dancing across the moon, Peter Berger helps our understanding by explaining that even as our increasingly technological world is perceived as increasingly secularized, such a perception would be incorrect. Suggests Berger, "secularization on the societal level is not necessarily linked to secularization on the level of individual consciousness. Certain religious institutions have lost power and influence . . . But both old and new religious beliefs and practices have nevertheless continued in the lives of individuals."[55] But Berger isn't satisfied with merely pointing out the persistence of the religious urge in individuals, and proposes that "*Counter-secularization* is at least as important a phenomenon in the contemporary world as secularization."[56] Thus, for Berger, even as modernity and secularization seem to have won the day, "counter-secularization" continues apace, both on the individual and societal levels, but in decidedly new forms.

50. Ferguson, *Aquarian Conspiracy*, 18–19.
51. Ibid., 18.
52. Ibid., 85.
53. Ibid., 363.
54. Ibid., 363.
55. Berger, *Desecularization*, 3.
56. Ibid., 6.

Reflective of these new forms, as Robert Fuller reports in *Spiritual but Not Religious*, a full 21 percent of the American population now considers itself deeply religious while actively eschewing any formal church affiliation.[57]

Echoing Berger, Morris Berman, in describing the modern period, suggests that "The story of the modern epoch, at least on the level of mind, is one of progressive disenchantment," which has resulted in a non-participation of humankind with nature, based on a "rigid distinction between observer and observed."[58] He contrasts this with a healthier postmodern or even occult worldview, with "its sense of everything being alive and interrelated," a world that is "sensual at its core." This, concludes Berman, "is the essence of reality."[59] Reenchantment of the postmodern, postsecular world, then, represents for Berman, the complete eradication of the "rigid distinction between observer and observed."

Berman goes on to suggest a singularity of all things, proposing that if and when we pollute a body of water, we are, in effect, causing it to lose its Mind (Berman's capitalization), and hence are beginning to move toward insanity ourselves. Such a degree of reenchantment of creation represents a "healthy move" (back) toward the wisdom of primitive peoples and is not, insists Berman, "opposed to the scientific intellect, but only to the inability of that world view to locate itself in a larger context."[60] This, then, is how Berman and other New Age thinkers like him square the circle and write of reenchanting the earth, while hunched over their Macs—desktop systems possessing more computing power than the Apollo project that landed men on the moon.

New Age Spirituality and Evangelical Pushback

But the dawning of the Age of Aquarius and its New Age spiritualities didn't arrive without pushback from various quarters, specifically from the conservatives of the evangelical world. John Drane, of the University of Aberdeen and Fuller Seminary, has been one such voice. He explains the New Age rationale for the rejection of the church and traditional Christianity in

57. Dreyer, "How to Remain Faithful," 5.

58. Berman, *Reenchantment*, 16.

59. Ibid., 177.

60. Ibid., 259.

two concise propositions. First, he articulates the likely assumptions of the typical New Ager.

> Our present predicament can be traced to mistakes made by West-
> ern thinkers in the course of the last 500 years, which in turn was
> rooted in the West's love affair with the rationality of the Greeks.
> This philosophy has led to the marginalization of human and spir-
> itual values, and an unhealthy preoccupation with a mechanistic,
> rationalistic, reductionistic worldview. There has been a profound
> loss of spiritual perception, and to resolve the present crisis that
> trend needs to be reversed. The recovery of spirituality must be a
> top priority.[61]

Sadly, for those still invested in traditional religions, specifically Christianity, Drane then suggests that the New Age community has weighed
traditional Christianity and found it wanting.

> The Christian church is a part of the old cultural establishment
> that actually created the present predicament . . . . For better or
> worse, therefore, Christianity is increasingly perceived as part of
> the problem, and for that reason it cannot also be part of the solu-
> tion: if spirituality is to be restored in today's world, it will have to
> come from somewhere else.[62]

Even so, Drane recognizes the unfortunate truth that "in the mainstream
Christian tradition, 'knowing God' has for the most part meant knowing
things about God, and quite often pretty abstruse and esoteric things, at
that."[63]

These sympathies aside, Drane, who earned his PhD in the study of
Gnosticism, sees direct linkages from historic Gnosticism to popular New
Age spiritualities. In illustration, Drane quotes a New Age acupuncturist
who perceives the spirit of the cosmos in his craft:

> The acupuncturist . . . Brings his patients back to health not only
> for their own sake and happiness, but so that the whole world may
> function properly. Every needle the acupuncturist twirls between
> his finders bears the heavy weight of universal harmony in its slim,
> pointed end.[64]

61. Drane, *What Is the New Age*, 15.
62. Ibid., 17.
63. Ibid., 58.
64. Ibid., 144.

Is it unfair to interpret this claim by the acupuncturist as a prescription for the ultimate redemption of the world in the prick of his needle? I think not, especially if he and his patients live in a newly reenchanted world in which the subject/object distinction has been largely erased and a belief in singularity reigns.

At this point, even the hardest-headed rationalists would no longer need a weatherman to see which way the wind was blowing. Perhaps we are all postmoderns now.

The Spear's Tip and the
Spiritual Formation of the Millennials

The aim of this review has been to paint a backdrop against which we may better understand the formation of the present generation of younger evangelicals.

While their baby boomer parents arguably came of age with one foot in modernity, the other in who-(then)-knew-what, their children—evangelicals of the X and, more likely, Y generations—have come of age with both feet planted (even if not so firmly) in *post*modernity. For these younger evangelicals, the painting of at least a tentative profile is possible, based upon our review in the pages above. Perhaps we may summarize the profile of the "typical" young evangelical with the following broad brush strokes. They:

1. do not embrace the certitudes of modernity, as did their parents and grandparents;

2. do not assume the hegemony of the either/or proposition;

3. do not assume the "regularity" and predictability of the universe;

4. do not assume that nature is based on "laws," the understanding of which will allow for nature's "management";

5. do not assume the existence of or inevitability of progress;

6. discount the subject/object distinction;

7. do not assume the fixedness of ethics, mores, or (nearly) anything else;

8. do not necessarily "honor" the status quo just due to its being the status quo;

9. do not believe that "the West is the best";

10. believe in and embrace diversity;

11. question the legitimacy of traditional religious and theological tenets—even those that have seemed to serve their predecessors well;

12. do not recognize the legitimacy of past patterns of worship, religious
life, or even spirituality just because they are established and storied;

13. often embrace lifestyles their elders would have deemed counter to
the faith;

14. are open to varied spiritual expressions and experiences;

15. are often open to alternative spiritual traditions and practices;

16. often find what they consider their parents' blend of faith and (conservative) social and political views noxious;

17. find "witnessing," as their parents might have done, unfashionable and
distasteful;

18. yearn for spiritual authenticity;

19. have little patience for Christianity as performance in the megachurch
mode;

20. want to experience knowing God, not simply "knowing about" God.

Leonard Sweet provides a helpful synopsis of these millennial traits in
his analysis of the current situation. He holds that "in the midst of one of
the greatest transitions in history—from modern to postmodern—Christian churches are owned lock, stock, and barrel by modernity. They have
clung to modern modes of thought and action."[65] Even worse, Sweet suggests, "Western Christianity went to sleep in a modern world governed by
the gods of reason and observation. It is awakening to a postmodern world
open to revelation and hungry for experience. Indeed, one of the last places
postmoderns expect to be 'spiritual' is the church."[66]

Sadly, we are reminded here of Willard's wistfully musings: "the evangelical form of Christian faith has achieved remarkable acceptance and
prominence in recent decades," but "we have not done well in four absolutely crucial areas":

- We haven't figured what the spiritual life is really like, inside and out.

---

65. Sweet, *Post-Modern Pilgrims*, 28.
66. Ibid., 29.

- We haven't dealt successfully with the challenge of transforming our characters into routine Christlikeness.

- We haven't succeeded in transforming our workplaces and vocations into extensions of the kingdom of Christ.

- We haven't learned how to live in God's power in every aspect of our lives.[67]

When weighing these evangelical shortcomings, as Willard does, one cannot help but wonder whether the success traded for them—"remarkable acceptance and prominence"—has been a wise or equitable trade. The legions of younger believers leaving the churches would indicate that perhaps the "acceptance and prominence" won by evangelicalism has been gained at a steep price.

If there is one single and identifiable phenomenon that would serve as the icon for this move of younger evangelicals out of their churches of origin, it is arguably the phenomenon of what is called "Emerging Church." In the following section we will review this phenomenon. It will not be exhaustive, for two reasons. First, others for whom the Emergent phenomenon is a central focus have already done this. Second, while many of these treatments of Emergent Christianity seem to consider it a likely answer to a greater problem, I do not. Instead, I find it more helpful to view the Emerging phenomenon not as a solution *to*, but rather as a symptom *of* a greater challenge. So, rather than dealing with Emergence as a solution to our drift from modernity into postmodernity, I have come to view it as evidence of our attempt to identify and solve a unique problem. Accordingly, I suspect that its ultimate and inevitable failure will doom its adherents to a likely cycle of repeated disappointment. Because of this view, we will necessarily review Emergence in the following section, but principally as a means to introduce what I suspect, and truly hope, can be the solution to the vexing problem evangelicalism and evangelicals face today, as our move into postmodernity is universally acknowledged and understood. Or at least recognized and grudgingly accepted.

67. Willard, "Preface," in Tomlinson, *Post Evangelical*, 12–13.

6

"I Left the Church Because . . ."
(Is Emergence the Answer?)

As is often the case, the canary in the coalmine setting off the alarm bells on the pulpits of evangelical leaders has been the youth. As we have seen in Hunter, Bass, and others, the steady erosion of Americans identifying themselves as (conservative) Protestants or evangelicals has yielded the growing number of "Nones"—those whose preferred box to check for their religious affiliation in surveys and questionnaires is "None." A recently released national study produced by the Public Religion Research Institute and Governance Studies at Brookings underscored these trends. The study reported that while a full 34 percent of baby boomers self-identify as religious conservatives, that percentage is halved for the youth, with only 17 percent of millennials self-identifying as religious conservatives. Meanwhile, while only 11 percent of the baby boomers classified themselves as non-religious, that number was doubled for millennials, with a full 22 percent considering themselves non-religious.[1]

Rachel Held Evans and Her Fifteen Theses

Rachel Held Evans, a popular millennial blogger, recently joined a chorus of like-minded young and articulate Christians reflecting on the problem of youth leaving the church. In fact, claims Evans, "Eight million twenty-somethings have left the church, and it seems like everyone is trying to

1. Jones et al., "Do Americans."

figure out why."[2] Held herself left the church at twenty-seven, and blogged fifteen reasons for having done so:

1. I left the church because I'm better at planning Bible studies than baby showers . . . but they only wanted me to plan baby showers.

2. I left the church because when we talked about sin, we mostly talked about sex.

3. I left the church because my questions were seen as liabilities.

4. I left the church because sometimes it felt like a cult, or a country club, and I wasn't sure which was worse.

5. I left the church because I believe the earth is 4.5 billion years old and that humans share a common ancestor with apes, which I was told was incompatible with my faith.

6. I left the church because sometimes I doubt, and church can be the worst place to doubt.

7. I left the church because I didn't want to be anyone's "project."

8. I left the church because it was often assumed that everyone in the congregation voted for Republicans.

9. I left the church because I felt like I was the only one troubled by stories of violence and misogyny and genocide in the Bible, and I was tired of people telling me not to worry about it because "God's ways are higher than our ways."

10. I left the church because of my own selfishness and pride.

11. I left the church because I knew I would never see a woman behind the pulpit, at least not in the congregation in which I grew up.

12. I left the church because I wanted to help people in my community without feeling pressure to convert them to Christianity.

13. I left the church because I had learned more from Oprah about addressing poverty and injustice than I had learned from 25 years of Sunday School.

14. I left the church because there are days when I'm not sure I believe in God, and no one told me that "dark nights of the soul" can be part of the faith experience.

2. Evans, "15 Reasons."

15. I left the church because one day they put signs out in the church lawn that said, "Marriage = 1 Man + 1 Woman: Vote Yes on Prop 1," and I knew the moment I saw them that I never wanted to come back.[3]

Reviewing Evans' theses, perhaps the initial thing that catches the eye is the attractive literary style with its preponderance of "I"s. Evans presents her theses employing the effective and attractive cadence of "I left . . . I left" through her fifteen points. Even so, it is an intriguing stylistic selection on her part, given that one of the consistent themes through much of the commentary regarding the state of the contemporary church is the alleged blight of consumerism that sullies nearly all things ecclesial.

In *Following Christ in a Consumer Society*, the Jesuit John F. Kavanaugh minces no words, warning that people of faith run the very real risk "that in achieving high economic freedom and productivity, we might fall into a more profound form of unfreedom: a slavery to consumerism itself."[4] Professors Eddie Gibbs and Ryan Bolger, both of Fuller Seminary, echo Kavanaugh's warnings. "Today, typically, individuals come to spirituality as shoppers. They consume spiritual experiences."[5] For this, the authors blame that twin-headed demon of advertising and marketing, concluding, "Churches that adopt a marketing approach treat their visitors as customers, numbers, and potential converts instead of simply as people."[6]

An irony may present itself here, for we would be correct in observing that among those Americans whose formation is most heavily and "successfully" fashioned by our consumerist culture are the millennials themselves. They are, by far, the most technologically connected, savvy, and marketed-to generation in American history. This observation is meant to neither undercut millennial condemnation of consumerism in the church nor diminish the insight and fervor of Evans' theses. Rather, it is meant merely to ask the question as to whether her fifteen points may themselves possess at least a few strands of this same consumerist DNA. That is to say, recognizing the passion of Evans' heartfelt points, might it be nonetheless possible to imagine them as disgruntled customer complaints, sadly swearing off her allegiance to a formerly beloved brand?

---

3. Ibid.

4. Kavanaugh, *Following Christ*, 35.

5. Gibbs and Bolger, *Emerging Churches*, 137.

6. Ibid., 137.

But perhaps for evangelical churches and their futures, the answer to these questions is secondary. This underscores the wisdom of Hunter's observation that the contemporary evangelical world is undergoing "an alteration in the cultural meaning of orthodoxy and, accordingly, an alteration in the cultural meaning of specific criteria of orthodoxy."[7] In other words, if Hunter is correct, perhaps attempting to parse Evans' fifteen points into either theological or cultural concerns is a fool's errand, because Evans and others like her are not simply underscoring points of difference in religious understanding, but tacitly engaged in altering "the cultural meaning of specific criteria of orthodoxy." Even so, and as Evans astutely points out, and as Hunter has also observed, "Conservative Protestantism has also cultivated a heritage of political and cultural intolerance."[8]

A constructive thought exercise might be to imagine a context in which Evans' fifteen reasons for leaving were reversed. In this new context, all of her concerns would be met. She would be asked to plan Bible studies not baby showers, discussion of sin would not exclusively focus on sex, her doubts and questions would be seriously addressed, her views on creation thoughtfully considered, and fellow parishioners would be disallowed from voting Republican. Would these changes then become reasons for Evans *staying in* rather than *leaving* the church? If so, then perhaps she—and we all—may be more the consumers of church and spirituality that we realize or would care to admit.

Even so, the strength of Evans' theses lies in the two implied underlying questions they convey. First, beyond whatever legitimate concerns she may be raising, Christians in general and evangelicals in particular must, especially in our postmodern period, begin to seriously grapple with the question, what is *church*? Or *the church*? Perhaps it is not inconsequential that when evangelical writers and thinkers speak and write on the contemporary church situation, they often speak to the need of "*doing* church differently." Leonard Sweet, for instance, sagely proposes, "The challenge for Postmodern Pilgrims is to give postmodern culture a 'witness': to 'do church' in ways that measure success by conceivings rather than consumings."[9]

Of course, the use of the phrase "doing church" may simply be shorthand for describing the task and process of running and managing a local faith assembly. On the other hand, could the phraseology also hint that

7. Hunter, *Evangelicalism*, 162.

8. Ibid., 129.

9. Sweet, *Post-Modern Pilgrims*, xxii.

the contemporary church, modern or post-, is an undertaking the success-ful execution of which depends upon "doing it" in a market-conscious and even salable manner? Maybe here we protest too much. But even so, if there is one truth postmodern thought has successfully deconstructed, it is that of the neutrality of language. Given this, it would seem that "*doing* church" might stand in contradistinction to "*being* church," as Sweet has wisely sug-gested elsewhere.

Second, once Evans articulates her fifteen points, she summarizes with a simple and heartfelt appeal, "Like every generation before ours and every generation after," she states, "we long for Jesus."[10] This yearning Evans expresses is easily the most appealing aspect of her observations. Indeed, culture, ecclesiology, and politics aside, it seems Evans and many of those for whom she gives voice yearn most for a church that will be catalytic to their formation into the image of Christ.

The Emerging Church

As a phenomenon, the Emerging Church movement has its enthusiasts as well as its detractors. Indeed, for some of the latter, the entire concept re-mains a frustrating abstraction of ill-defined and amorphously articulated complaints about the present state of, especially, the evangelical churches. To this point, millennials DeYoung and Kluck, in their fair, and at times hu-morous, *Why We're Not Emergent*, observe, "The Emerging church thrives on eschewing definition, of itself and of its theology."[11] Even so, because the Emergent phenomenon is contemporaneous with the exodus of millions of youths from traditional evangelical churches, a definition of the Emergent phenomenon must be attempted. In their attempt to define the Emerging Church, Gibbs and Bolger suggest, "Emerging churches are communities that practice the way of Jesus within postmodern cultures."[12]

The authors helpfully follow up with an instructive list of nine "practices" of the Emerging Church. According to the authors, Emerging churches "1) identify with the life of Jesus, 2) transform the secular realm, and 3) live highly communal lives. Because of these three activities, they 4) welcome the stranger, 5) serve with generosity, 6) participate as producers,

---

10. Evans, "15 Reasons."
11. DeYoung and Kluck, *Why We're Not*, 78.
12. Gibbs and Bolger, *Emerging Churches*, 44.

7) create as created beings, 8) lead as a body, and 9) take part in spiritual activities."[13]

Armed with these points of outline, I would suggest that the following generalization may be made. The Emerging Church phenomenon is one significant manifestation of a generation of dissatisfied young Christians for whom evangelicalism—arguably, the Siamese twin of Enlightenment modernity—no longer adequately speaks to their *post*modern reality. Paralleling this thought, Emergent spokesman Kevin Corcoran reports that many Emergent Christians are calling for "a Christianity beyond belief. The idea is that committing oneself to concrete Christian beliefs places oneself in the primordial waters of modernism and the pretentious grip of the Enlightenment ideal."[14]

Phyllis Tickle explains, "Emergence Christianity is, first and foremost, deinstitutionalized." She amplifies this thought by further announcing, "Deinstitutionalization is likewise a prime characteristic that Emergence Christianity shares completely and unequivocally with the culture at large."[15] Suggesting (with no obvious sense of irony) that Emergence is a movement solidifying around the phenomenon of deinstitutionalization, Tickle chronicles a movement whose adherents are techno-savvy, comfortable with paradox, eschew an either/or approach to life, favor a both/and posture, and have retreated from doctrinal and dogmatic postures, particularly as related to their faith.[16]

Peter Rollins, one of the more thoughtful Emergent writers, echoes Tickle's point by proposing that the Emergent movement demands a new definition of orthodoxy. Emergent orthodoxy, for Rollins, focuses on "being in the world," and, as Corcoran explains, "The postmodern turn for Christians is, therefore a turn away from Christianity as *believing* or *knowing* certain things and a turn toward Christianity as opening oneself up to a transformative *event*."[17]

Emergent spokesman, and arguably the movement's godfather, Brian McLaren describes his own Emergent embracing of the faith and the Lord in his widely read *A Generous Orthodoxy*:

---

13. Ibid., 44–45.

14. McKnight et al., *Church in the Present Tense*, 13.

15. Tickle, *Emergence Christianity*, 130.

16. Ibid., 131–132.

17. McKnight, et al., 13.

I am a Christian because I have confidence in Jesus Christ—in all his dimensions (those I know, and those I don't). I trust Jesus. I think Jesus is right because I believe God was in Jesus in an unprecedented way. Through Jesus I have entered into a real, experiential relationship with God as Father, and I have received God's Spirit into my life. I have experienced the love of God through Jesus, and as the old hymn says, "Love so amazing, so divine, demands my heart, my life, my all." As I seek to follow Jesus as my leader, guide, and teacher, I believe I am experiencing life in its fullest dimensions—full of joy and love, and, yes, full of struggle and challenge, too. For all these reasons and more, I love Jesus. I believe Jesus embraces me, and you, and the whole world in the love of God.[18]

McLaren's Emergent creed is helpful in underscoring the longing Rollins also conveys, and the deep yearning many Emergents express, for personal transformation on a level that far transcends modernity's promise of knowing *about* God, to a genuine *knowing* of God. McLaren, for his part, sums up his generous orthodoxy with his own attractive and heartfelt expression of desire to enter into and live in the love of Christ.

In Emergent writers one sees dual forces at work. First, there is the disillusionment with the unmet promises of modernity and with an exhausted evangelicalism, joined at its hip. Second, as Evans so compellingly expressed, "deep down, we long for Jesus." This desired retreat from perceived modernistic creeds and belief systems to simple and sincere engagement with Jesus in the present world is expressed by Corcoran, who explains that for many Emergents the "gospel is radically *this-worldly*," and its living out in one's life is real to the extent that one engages in "God-love and neighbor-love."[19] This grappling with gospel—its definition, meaning, and application—is in fact central to an understanding of Emergence itself.

Scot McKnight: The Gospel of King Jesus

Scot McKnight, the North Park biblical theologian, is a central figure in the contemporary grappling with the gospel to discern its present meaning for followers of Jesus, and for the world in which they live. N. T. Wright, writing the preface to McKnight's *The King Jesus Gospel*, observes that "the

18. McLaren, *Generous Orthodoxy*, 77.
19. McKnight et al., *Church in the Present*, xiv.

movement that has long called itself 'evangelical' is in fact better labeled 'soterian,'" because while "we have thought we were talking about 'the gospel' . . . we were concentrating on 'salvation.'"[20] This parsing of gospel and salvation is the central crux of McKnight's thesis. And this effort not only has its pedigree in postmodern thought, but also holds promise for a way forward for disillusioned Emergent believers to whom Evans and others have given voice.

In his attempt to disentangle gospel from salvation, the first point McKnight seeks to establish is the identification of the tradition within classical evangelicalism of equating salvation primarily with a personal decision. Indeed, as he points out, "I believe we are focused on the wrong thing. Most of evangelicalism today obsesses with getting someone to make a *decision*; the apostles, however, were obsessed with making *disciples.*"[21] For McKnight, this evangelical decisionism has dual and related consequences. First, focusing on a punctiliar decision and calling it salvation "appears to distort spiritual formation." The second consequence of this focus on decision has, in McKnight's thinking, yielded a resultant distortion of the formational process, which has allowed for a loss of "*at least 50% of those who make decisions.*"[22]

To rectify this, McKnight recommends recognizing that the salvation message and the gospel story are not identical. Indeed, suggests McKnight, "the 'gospel' of the New Testament cannot be reduced to the Plan of Salvation. Instead, the Plan of Salvation . . . Flows out of (and is founded upon) the Story of Israel and the Story of Jesus." Continuing in this thought, McKnight proposes that "the more we submerge 'salvation' into the larger idea of 'gospel,' the more robust will become our understanding of salvation."[23]

If McKnight is correct, we can conclude that traditional evangelicalism may have a soteriology problem. Perhaps tying itself for so long to a modernistic paradigm has weakened evangelicalism's soteriological understanding as well as its message. In short, modernity's model of point-in-time, either/or understanding of reality has set the tone for evangelicalism's understanding and presentation of salvation as principally a punctiliar, decisional event. The postmodern preference for process, for both/and versus either/or, and for a holistic versus linear understanding of the nature of all

20. McKnight, *King Jesus Gospel*, 12.

21. Ibid., 18.

22. Ibid., 20.

23. Ibid., 39.

things, salvation included, may in fact reveal a thinness in the traditional evangelical understanding of salvation. The poor "sticking power" of the decisional paradigm, as McKnight has already underscored, would seem to buttress this point. In a further indictment of a thin evangelical soteriology, McKnight criticizes what he labels the "salvation culture" as primarily focusing on the hope and promise of a *personal* salvation.[24]

This traditional evangelical framing of salvation as a principally punctiliar and personal event has, for McKnight, had dire consequences. We have already seen his indictment of this model's poor record related to its substandard showing in yielding long-term spiritual formation. Even worse, concludes McKnight, is that when the Plan of Salvation is separated from the full and robust gospel story, "the plan almost always becomes abstract, propositional, logical, rational, and philosophical."[25] While such a plan is fit, perhaps, for a primarily rationalistic and modernistic generation living in a coldly disenchanted world, it seems to have proven offensive and off-putting for their postmodern offspring embracing *journey, irony, paradox,* and *spiritual enlightenment.*

Thus, for a younger generation whose philosophical and attitudinal formation has been successfully fashioned by a relentless media culture crafted by poets, writers, entertainers, advertisers, and thinkers prophesying from the spear's tip, the classical, modernistic evangelical understanding of salvation may no longer be a fit. Their exodus from evangelical churches underscores this point.

Perhaps we can summarize here by concluding that a young cohort for whom don Juan was right, and for whom Castaneda actually flew, now populates the evangelical churches. And whether Castaneda flew, carrying the boulder to which he was anchored, or flew untethered is moot to this demographic. I recall my art professor once being queried by a fellow student. The artist stared mute at his boots for some time, and then finally looked up and addressed the student and her question. "I can't give you an answer," he replied, "because your question isn't good enough." Similarly, it seems that for a growing number of younger evangelicals, traditional evangelicalism itself may be the answer to a question that is no longer "good enough." Put another way, if the expression and embrace of classical evangelicalism is the religious and logical response to a *modern zeitgeist*—a modern zeitgeist we are now jettisoning—does either the expression or the

24. Ibid., 30.
25. Ibid., 62.

embrace still make sense? A growing number of younger evangelicals are voting no with their feet.

For McKnight, separating the Plan of Salvation from the gospel is so critical that if we fail to do so, we will ultimately fail to comprehend the story of Jesus and its full meaning for the church, for the world, and for ourselves. McKnight emphasizes that while our Plan of Salvation has typically focused on a personal and individual concept of salvation, the full-orbed and robust *gospel of Jesus* is different. He proposes that from the beginning of the biblical story the world is depicted as a cosmic temple, and that "God places humans in his temple, but when he does he makes humans his Eikons, the God-bearers, and their responsibility is to relate to God, self, others, and the world *as co-rulers with God and as mediators of God's presence in God's cosmic temple.*"[26]

It is precisely at this point, and *in* this point, that the seed of the solution to evangelicalism's current challenges are to be found. In finding the classical evangelical Plan of Salvation within the greater gospel story, McKnight has potentially cut the conversionism of traditional evangelicalism free of its modernistic moorings. Will McKnight's gospel, now free of its historic individualistic, punctiliar, and perhaps even overly juridical understanding, be better able to speak to a younger generation of would-be believers, who themselves have also largely been cut and untethered from modernity's moorings? McKnight hopes so. So do I.

The good news is that in drawing attention to the alleged thinness of the traditional evangelical Plan of Salvation, and in proposing a far more robust understanding of *gospel*—one that speaks to a new, postmodern *zeitgeist*, and is thoroughly expansive to the point of bearing cosmic ramifications—McKnight is neither alone nor original. Though eclipsed for centuries by a triumphant modern, Western rationalism, the historic church knew, at its genesis, a gospel that was neither thin nor tamed by an imperial, either/or empiricism. Indeed, this muscular, full-bodied, and arguably even wild and untamable gospel is not and cannot be managed or defanged, especially by a modernity in serious ebb.

Instead, this historic gospel, while hospitable to the rationality of humans created in the image and likeness of God, also vibrates with the dark, awful, and impenetrable mystery of a nonetheless knowable deity. And it is this knowledge of and communion with this relational deity that has the power to reenchant the world and indeed the entire cosmos. It has too the

26. Ibid., 137. Italics original.

power to make the hearts of mere men and women fit habitations for a holy God. This same divine power has, as well, been historically understood as having the power to make of these same men and women saints who stride the earth as gods, redeeming and making holy the contexts and people they touch. It is this gospel and this God for whom Rachel Evans and her generation yearns. Perhaps their exodus from evangelical churches underscores the thinness, as McKnight writes, of the Plan of Salvation, along with the vacuousness of the managed, programmatic, and modernistic church extravaganzas that have failed them.

In the next chapter we will explore the gospel of the ancient church and propose that the remedy to the present hollowing out of the evangelical movement is not simply an insistence that "everything must change." And it certainly is not to be found in yet another repackaging and presentation of a "new" evangelicalism. Instead, the answer lies in a journey to the East, back to the future, back to a gospel of mystery and grandeur, and fit for the redemption of humanity, the earth, and the entire cosmos. So let us begin this journey to explore and reclaim the ancient heart of our gospel and our faith. In doing so we welcome mystery, the tension of the already/not yet, and the potential discomfort of embracing a faith so large, so expansive, and so awe-full that it eclipses our Enlightenment-bred Western rationality and tradition. Ours, indeed, is an ancient, premodern, *Eastern* religion.

7

Back to the Future
and the Faith of the Fathers
Theosis

WHEN OUR GROWING FAMILY left our small evangelical church, as related in chapter 1, the months following were filled with an unhappy migration from church to church. At that point, I entered a protracted study of the patristics, seeking answers to my plaguing questions, central to which was a deep desire to explore the meaning of "church" as traditionally understood. This left me with a desire to explore the Eastern Orthodox Church. So one Sunday we went on a "field trip" and entered another world. As we ventured into that small Orthodox church, we had little idea of what to expect, and no idea as to how our lives would soon change.

As we stepped across the threshold, into the darkened sanctuary, clouds of sweet incense wafted through the air, icons covering the walls. The iconostasis, at the front of the church, was a wall of beautiful iconography and woodwork. The stage, or what I would come to know as the altar, was equipped with lampstands and canopied in hanging lamps. It was certainly different, exotic even. But my enduring response was much deeper than these superficial perceptions. As I stepped into this sensory feast, a single, surprising recognition sprang to mind as the entire panorama and sense of *mysterium tremendum* took my breath away.

"So *this* is where I've been all these years," I thought to myself. I sat—and stood—through the service in awe, bowled over by the organic primitivism and beauty of the Liturgy of St. John Chrysostom. I recognized, as the liturgy progressed, that the Exchange Formula of which I was becoming aware in patristic theology sat at its core. In this "exchange," God himself, through his Son, exchanged our life for his, and in doing so was inviting us to share in who he is—in his very divinity—though not by nature but by grace.

"So, I wasn't '*off*,'" I mused. I hadn't been lost in the high weeds of my own post-evangelical heresy! Indeed, what I had read of the partaking of the divine nature was at the core of this ancient church. *Theosis* wasn't a so-teriological anomaly or quirk. It wasn't a fringe, disputed theology. Rather, it was the *bedrock* of our ancient Christian faith. I was *home*. But what does this truncated telling of my personal journey have to do with the state of evangelicalism at the close of the modern age? A lot, as I will suggest below.

Theosis: The Deification of the Christian

Georgios Mantzaridis, Chair of Moral Theology and Christian Sociology at the University of Thessaloniki, suggests that the church is the "'new build-ing' formed by Christ through His incarnation and through His 'recapitula-tion' of all things to Himself."[1] This "new building," professor Mantzaridis writes, has a singular purpose: "The Church's aim is the deification of its members." Mantzaridis then quotes St. Gregory Palamas, of the fourteenth century, who defined the church as the "communion of deification."[2] These propositions of "theosis," and especially "deification," can be alarming and foreign to our ears and theological experience, and they deserve definition.

But first, perhaps as a bridge between this Eastern Christian theological understanding with the Western, we can refer to the *Catechism of the Catholic Church*. This official Catholic document and resource describes the vocation of all Christians as being to progress "toward ever more intimate union with God. This union is called 'mystical' because it participates in the mystery of Christ through the sacraments."[3] The Catechism then explains that "It is in the Church, in communion with all the baptized, that the Christian fulfills his vocation."[4] Finally, underscoring that humanity's perfect destiny lay in union with God, the Catechism states, "Constituted in a state of holiness, man was destined to be fully 'divinized' by God in glory." Unfortunately, as the Catechism explains, this destiny was derailed. "Seduced by the devil, he

1. Mantzaridis, *Deification of Man*, 57.
2. Ibid., 57.
3. *Catechism of the Catholic Church*, 543.
4. Ibid., 545.

(man) wanted to 'be like God,' but 'without God, before God, and not in accordance with God.'"[5] With this input from the ancient church, both East and West, we can begin to recognize the purpose of the church as far more than "evangelizing" or embracing the "Plan of Salvation."

While acknowledging and being grateful for the grace of God imputed into the community of the faithful in recent history—through the work and experience of, say, the Pentecostals and also the evangelicals—we do well to recognize that the origins of the church predate Aimee Semple McPherson, or even Luther and Calvin. In fact, the church—the church of all who would identify as Christians—had its origins in the East, rising from the rubble of a crumbling Roman Empire. As such, this ancient church largely constructed its articulation of the faith while engaged in a life-or-death struggle against heterodoxy and heresies.

Even as we see that the ancient church understood (and understands) its mission not as primarily about evangelism or church growth, but rather about the deification of its members—by bringing them into union with God—we must recognize, in a parallel fashion, that the ancient church also defines or understands salvation in a far different way than do most modern evangelicals. Indeed, Scot McKnight's noble efforts to broaden the evangelical understanding of salvation beyond the Plan of Salvation, were anticipated by the church fathers.

Again, as we move forward to explore this ancient, premodern, and patristic understanding of salvation, we may be surprised to discover a soteriological model and understanding that parallels a postmodern sense—graced with process, pilgrimage, journey, enlightenment and, yes, even paradox and irony—currency of the realm of many young postmodern evangelicals. Archimandrite Christoforos Stavropoulos offers a helpful preliminary introduction to the ancient Christian understanding of salvation:

> In the Holy Scriptures, where God Himself speaks, we read of a unique call directed to us. God speaks to us human beings clearly and directly and He says: "I said, 'You are gods, sons of the Most high, all of you'" (Ps 82:6 and John 10:34). Do we hear that voice? Do we understand the meaning of this calling? Do we accept that we should in fact be on a journey, a road that leads to Theosis? As human beings we each have this one, unique calling, to achieve Theosis.[6]

---

5. Ibid., 398.

6. Russell, *Fellow Workers*, 13.

This proposed answer to our initial question, "What *is* the church and what is its purpose?," suggesting that the church's primary goal is to affect the divinization of its members, stands in stark contrast to the answer that might be offered in most evangelical churches today. In fact, would it be unfair to conclude, from an examination of the structure and programmatic focus of many evangelical churches today, that more than a few may be existing simply to exist? Or perhaps just to *grow*? Certainly, persistence in existence along with some degree of growth is necessary to supply the energy and verve needed to relate to a needy world. Even so, existing primarily to self-perpetuate or even just to grow may be, as the sociologist Max Weber once suggested, a warning sign of encroaching necrosis.

If the central mission of the church is to create deified members who are being intentionally formed away from conformity to the world, and into union with God—with theosis as their holy destiny—then a reconsideration of this mission may force a redefinition of church and its work. It may also suggest that a rethinking of what it means to be saved and to be a Christian would be productive. With this rethinking in mind, let us look more closely at churchly mission, as stated by representatives of the ancient church.

Theosis and the Fathers of the Church

While terms such as "deification," "theosis," and even "union" are not commonly heard in evangelical churches today, these terms were not at all foreign to the primitive contexts that existed at the genesis of our faith. In fact, when significant early church fathers described our faith and the intended ultimate destiny of our lives of faith, they often did so in what sounds to us today as startling language.

St. Irenaeus of Lyons, a student of Polycarp, who was himself a disciple of St. John, the disciple of Jesus, lived and ministered in the second century. He spent much of his ministry struggling for the faith and in the defense of the faithful, his central written work being *Against Heresies*, written in opposition to Gnosticism. In book 5 of that work, St. Irenaeus describes the true faith and its "steadfast Teacher, the word of God, our Lord Jesus Christ, who did, through His transcendent love, become what we are, that He might bring us to be even what He is Himself."[7]

---

7. St. Irenaeus, *Against Heresies*, 526.

Clement of Alexandria, a second-century church father revered as a saint by both the Eastern Orthodox and Eastern Catholic Churches, wrote, "The Word of God became man so that you too may learn from a man how it is even possible for a man to become a god."[8]

St. Basil the Great, Bishop of Caesarea, also living and ministering in the fourth century, wrote, "From the Holy Spirit there is the likeness of God, and the highest of all things to be desired, to become God."[9]

Perhaps an even more pointed proposition comes to us from St. Athanasius, bishop of Alexandria, who battled the Arian heresies. The saint, in section 54 of his masterwork, *On the Incarnation*, writes of Jesus, "For He was made man that man might be made God."[10]

In a parallel fashion, St. Gregory of Nazianzus, who lived and ministered in the fourth century, exhorted his flock, "Let us become as Christ is, since Christ became as we are; let us become gods for his sake, since he became man for our sake."[11]

St. Cyril of Alexandria, living and ministering as the fourth century ended, is thought by many to have been the most important theologian of the fifth century. Reflecting on 2 Peter 1:4, the bishop of Alexandria taught that we are "called to participate in divinity. Although Jesus Christ alone is by nature God, all people are called to become God 'by participation.' Through such participation, we become likenesses of Christ and perfect images of God the Father."[12]

Finally, St. Maximus the Confessor, who also struggled against heresies, suffering torture for the faith in the seventh century, wrote in his famous *Ambigua*, "God and man are paradigms of one another, that as much as God is humanized to man through love for mankind, so much has man been able to deify himself to God through love."[13]

The patristic scholar Norman Russell summarizes these truths articulated by these patristic fathers:

> From Irenaeus in the second century to Maximus in the seventh many of the Fathers see theosis as summarizing the very purpose of the Incarnation—the loving self-emptying of God (kenosis) evoking

8. Russell, *Fellow Workers*, 39.

9. Clendenin, *Eastern Orthodox*, 117.

10. St. Athanasius, *Incarnation of the Word*, 65.

11. Russell, *Fellow Workers*, 39.

12. Clendenin, *Eastern Orthodox*, 128.

13. Russell, *Fellow Workers*, 39.

a fervent human response (theosis), the divinization of the human person mirroring the humanization of the divine Word.[14]

If we are correctly understanding these church fathers, and if Russell, in turn, is correct in seeing theosis, or the divinization of the human person, as the ultimate *telos* or purpose of the incarnation, this may mean only one thing: we're not in modernistic Kansas anymore, and our church fathers are professing a soteriological reality that dramatically eclipses the Four Spiritual Laws. We will explore this eclipse in depth, below, but first we must be very clear about two key points.

First, many serious Christians were introduced to God's grace via tools such as the Four Spiritual Laws. Hence, we are not to diminish or discount an expression of God's merciful grace in whatever form it manifests. Rather, we are to be humbly grateful for his enduring mercy toward us, and thus stand in awe of God's obvious employment of this simple tract, and means like it, as channels of his grace.

Even so, if Scot McKnight and others are correct, this tool with which most evangelicals (and former evangelicals) are familiar may be a good example of an important though truncated expression of the Plan of Salvation. Eclipsing this expression, suggests McKnight, is the overarching *gospel of Jesus*. Again, as we have seen above, McKnight and others understand the Plan of Salvation as being contained within the greater *gospel of Jesus*. Likewise, it follows that if we are to enjoy the fullness of God's grace and purpose for his entire creation, we must broaden our understanding of holy *telos* from the Plan of Salvation to the gospel story of Jesus.

Defining Theosis, or Divinization

Second, it is necessary to carefully explore and understand the definition of theosis, or divinization. As might be expected for such an arresting concept, we will find that it is just as important to be clear as to what theosis is *not* as to ascertain what it is.

Russell helpfully defines, or rather, describes the concept of theosis:

> All theological language is rooted in metaphor. Redemption, for example, means literally "being ransomed or bought back." Salvation means "being made safe and whole." Theosis, or "becoming god," implies more than redemption or salvation. It is not simply

14. Ibid., 40.

the remedying of our defective human state. It is nothing less than our entering into partnership with God, our becoming fellow workers with him (1 Cor 3:9) for the sake of bringing the divine economy to its ultimate fulfillment.[15]

He then continues by exploring the word theosis itself, noting its derivation from the Greek verb *theoo*, meaning "to make god."[16] It is this term, explains Russell, that had by the time of St. Maximus the Confessor, in the seventh century, become the standard theological designator in the Christian East describing what was held out as the ultimate destiny of the believer.[17]

Emil Bartos, the Romanian Orthodox scholar, grants that "although the term theosis is not found in the Bible, the Fathers created it chiefly in their Christological and soteriological disputes with the heresies of their day." Bartos then proposes that theosis, or "deification is a divine gift and the ultimate and supreme goal for human existence. It involves an intimate union of the human being with the Triune God."[18]

From an unexpected source in the West comes a helpful definition, or rather, description of theosis, by Baptist scholar Clark Pinnock. Pinnock describes Christian salvation as being multifaceted and touching on key truths such as new birth, justification, and sanctification—all with the goal of "glorification and union with God," and suggests, "To think of salvation in this way is to "recover what early theologians called *theosis*."[19]

Coupling these contemporary descriptions or definitions of theosis with the patristic citations above, we may draw several important conclusions, along with a number of key observations.

Theosis in Patristic Apologetics and Christology

First, as is obvious from these patristic citations, the concept of theosis of the believer was, for the church fathers, a central and assumed soteriological theme and goal. As such, theosis is not a new development or recent theological innovation that must be shoehorned into the teachings of the fathers or retrofitted into their ancient faith. Instead, not only was the concept of divinization present at the earliest stages of patristic thought, but

15. Ibid., 36.
16. Ibid., 36.
17. Ibid. 36.
18. Bartos, *Deification*, 7.
19. Pinnock, *Flame*, 150.

also, as we shall see below, it has developed and then matured through the centuries. Indeed, the very concept of theosis came under intense scrutiny and became subject of bitter theological disputes, ultimately being declared orthodox and central to the teachings of the church at the time of St. Gregory Palamas in the fifteenth century.

Second, it should be recognized that the theology of divinization was developed, as we can see from the dating of the patristic quotes above, through the eras during which the church battled fierce heretical foes. In other words, the church doctrine and understanding of theosis developed during those periods in which it wrestled strenuously to craft and solidify the meaning, parameters, and articulation of Christian orthodoxy. This is no small or coincidental point, particularly as it relates to the concept or theology of divinization. Vladimir Lossky, arguably the most influential Orthodox thinker of the twentieth century, has shown that for these apologetic fathers, divinization was not a proposed theology they set out to prove in the course of their work. Instead, it was quite the opposite. As Lossky points out, divinization, or theosis, was assumed as the ultimate destiny of the believer, and it was on the foundation of this assumption that the fathers built their theological systems of the incarnation and Christology. Lossky explains,

> The Fathers of the "Christological centuries," though they formulated a dogma of Christ the God-Man, never lost sight of the question concerning our union with God. The usual arguments they bring up against unorthodox doctrines refer particularly to the fullness of our union, our deification, which becomes impossible if one separates the two natures of Christ, as Nestorius did, or if one only ascribes to Him one divine nature, like the Monophysites, or if one curtails one part of human nature, like Apollinarius, or if one only sees in Him a single divine will and operation, like the Monothelites. "What is not assumed, cannot be deified"—this is the argument to which the Fathers continually return.[20]

Rather than patristic Christology being crafted to prove the thesis of divinization, divinization was assumed by the fathers to be the ultimate human *telos* and destiny. Their orthodox Christology, then, was developed as a fitting support to that assumption. Sounding a similar note, the Romanian scholar Emil Bartos underscores and emphasizes the linkage between the christological developments of the early fathers and the theology

20. Lossky, *Mystical Theology*, 154–55.

of the divinization of the believer. Referencing the contemporary work of Father Dumitru Staniloae, Bartos points out that Father Staniloae built his own theology of divinization on the theological timbers that were logged, milled, and seasoned at Chalcedon.

> Therefore the foundation for his theology of deification arises from the question of the *communicatio idiomatum* of the two natures in Christ . . . Thus in conformity with the formula affirmed at Chalcedon, the subject is one in Christ but his natures are two. The communion of these two natures was called hypostatic union, by hypostasis being meant first of all the integrity of reality. One of Staniloae's key assertions is that, in the act of incarnation, the Son of God Himself entered into maximal union with us, and thus into the plane of our common experience . . . Hence Christ is not a twofold hypostasis, but the same hypostasis has a twofold quality: of God and man. This understanding shows both the value of the human persons and the capability of human nature to receive the Logos as hypostasis.[21]

What we see here is an example of the theology of deification dynamically related to the doctrine of orthodox Christology. In other words, in Staniloae's model, were it not for the hypostasis of the God-man, Jesus the Christ, human deification would not be possible. It is thus only through the mystery of the incarnation that the mystery of human deification is possible, or perhaps one could even say, *necessary*. In this understanding, both Bartos and Staniloae were anticipated by St. Maximus the Confessor.

> For St. Maximus the incarnation (sarkosis) and deification (theosis) correspond to one another; they mutually imply each other. God descends to the world and becomes man, and man is raised toward divine fullness and becomes god, because this union of two natures, the divine and the human, has been determined in the eternal counsel of God, and because it is the final end for which the world has been created out of nothing.[22]

Fuller theologian Veli-Matti Kärkkäinen agrees with this linkage between patristic Christology and divinization, specifically adding the anthropological variable.

> It should be clear now that for Palamas as well as Athanasius and the other fathers, any diminution of the divine or human nature of

21. Bartos, *Deification*, 168.

22. Lossky, *Mystical Theology*, 136.

Christ is not just a question of theology, it relates to anthropology as well. If Christ himself were a creature, then he could not have brought about union with God.[23]

Finally, we can also see in Russell's thinking a catalytic linkage between the incarnation and the potential deification of humanity.

The critical event which has made this unification possible is the Incarnation. Through the Incarnation, Christ manifested God's love, inaugurating a new age in which the corrupting principle introduced into our nature by the Fall was banished . . . Christ did not simply restore human nature to its pristine state. He opened up new possibilities for it. By his natural *sarkosis*, or "enfleshing," he brought us a supernatural *theosis*, or "engodding."[24]

Theosis and the Patristic "Exchange Formula"

A careful reading of these references provides more than a hint of the idea of exchange that is occurring here, via the incarnation, between God and humanity. In fact, as Russell elaborates, the incarnational mystery, and the divinization of humanity, which it makes possible, was described by the fathers as the "Exchange Formula."[25] Professor Daniel Keating echoes Russell, elaborating that the "formula of exchange" is the common phrase describing this God-human trade, in which "the eternal Son of God became what we are so that we could become what he is."[26] Russell continues on this point, referencing St. Ephrem the Syrian, who taught that "He gave us divinity" and "we gave him humanity."[27] Russell continues, citing Gosta Hallonsten, who suggests that this Exchange Formula has remained "simply a 'theological theme' in the West, while in the East it expresses 'a comprehensive doctrine that encompasses the whole of the economy of salvation.'" Therefore, continues Hallonsten, "A real doctrine of theosis . . . Is to be found only in the East."[28] At the time in which he was writing, Hallonsten may have been

23 Kärkkäinen, *One with God*, 29.

24. Russell, *Fellow Workers*, 45.

25. Ibid., 39.

26. Keating, *Deification and Grace*, 11.

27. Russell, *Fellow Workers*, 24.

28. Ibid., 38.

correct. Happily, however, as we shall see below, there are positive signs that this unfortunate state is in the process of being rectified.

Following the above two points, there is a third conclusion to be drawn here. It is that for the fathers of the church divinization was not a unique grace reserved for an elite core of privileged believers. Instead, quite to the contrary, and citing St. Basil the Great, the Eastern scholar Panayiotis Nellas writes,

> The true greatness of man is not found in his being the highest biological existence, a "rational" or "political" animal, but in his being a "deified animal," in the fact that he constitutes a created existence "which has received the command to become a god."[29]

Indeed, continues Nellas, it is in this command to "become a god" wherein lies "the greatness of man . . . His destiny, his appointed end."[30]

We see this same understanding of the catholicity of divinization as the desired end of all humanity in Mantzaridis, who describes deification as "God's greatest gift to man and the ultimate goal of human existence."[31] Interestingly, Russell cites Archbishop Anastasios, who goes beyond the thought of theosis as a privilege open to all humanity. Indeed, the Archbishop goes so far as to insist upon theosis as a "fundamental human right."[32]

We have seen, thus far, the doctrine of theosis, defined as union with God, and an exchange of God's divinity for our humanity. We have also seen how the doctrine was knit into the very fabric of the patristic understanding of the incarnation and the fathers' formulation of orthodox Christology and soteriology. Finally, we have seen how the fathers and teachers of the church have consistently instructed that divinization is the intended destiny of all humanity, rather than just an elect few.

What Theosis Is Not

Having reached this point, it is now appropriate to identify two key things that theosis is *not*. A full understanding of these points is needed, lest both proponents and opponents of this important doctrine needlessly clash. Just

---

29. Nellas, *Deification in Christ*, 30.

30. Ibid., 30.

31. Mantzaridis, *Deification of Man*, 12.

32. Russell, *Fellow Workers*, 173.

as important, understanding is also needed so as to insure against grave anthropological and theological error.

The first thing the patristic, orthodox doctrine of divinization is *not*, is a proposition for the mingling of the divine with the human essence. As clearly set forth by the holy fathers, the doctrine of theosis does not entail or imply confusion or mingling of the essence of God and human. Kärkkäinen, like many others, emphasizes this point, referencing St. Macarius, who taught that "persons to be deified . . . retain their own identity (i.e., do not overstep the distinction between God and humans)."[33] Kärkkäinen also cites St. Maximus, who explains that a person "who becomes obedient to God in all things hears God saying: 'I said; you are gods' (John 10:34); he then is God and is called 'God' not by nature or by relation but by divine decree and grace."[34] Lossky's explanation on this point is more specific, while also being more layered.

> The union to which we are called is neither hypostatic—as in the case of the human nature of Christ—nor substantial, as in that of the three divine Persons: it is union with God in His energies, or union by grace making us participate in the divine nature, without our essence becoming the essence of God. In deification we are by grace . . . All that God is by nature, save only identity of nature . . . We remain creatures while becoming God by grace, as Christ remained God in becoming man by the Incarnation.[35]

Keating underscores this important clarification, humorously clarifying, "deification does not mean the change of our nature into something other than it is—it is not an ontological promotion."[36] In other words, as St. Maximus concludes, "nothing at all changes its nature by being deified."[37] Again, in so saying, St. Maximus is simply echoing the fathers' understanding of theosis that, while the divine God-man is God by nature, we humans participate in the divine nature only by grace.

Emil Bartos, the Romanian scholar we met above, synopsizes this caution by explaining that according to Eastern theology, "'becoming god' does not mean an identification with God's divine nature (essence) but

---

33. Kärkkäinen, *One with God*, 27.
34. Ibid., 27.
35. Lossky, *Mystical Theology*, 87.
36. Keating, *Deification and Grace*, 110.
37. Ibid., 110.

rather something experienced by adoption, by grace, and by imitation."[38] Finally, to underscore this important point, we turn to a Western, Protestant, though sympathetic source, Daniel B. Clendenin:

> All of the Eastern theologians, both ancient and modern, uniformly and categorically repudiate any hint of pantheism. Whatever it means to "become god," the essence of human nature is not lost. In this sense human theosis is a relative rather than an absolute transformation. There is a real and genuine union of the believer with God, but it is not a literal fusion or confusion in which the integrity of human nature is compromised. Orthodoxy consistently rejects the idea that humans participate in the essence or nature of God.[39]

From these references, along with the clear tradition of the church of the East, it is safe to conclude that the doctrine of theosis cannot be regarded as promoting the confusion of the human with the divine essence, unless one gravely misunderstands the doctrine or its proponents, or confuses it with contemporary misunderstandings or heresies.

Theosis and Scriptural Support

Turning from this initial critical issue, we are ready to explore the second reality which theosis is not. Put simply, it is not a doctrine without biblical support. Even so, as Kärkkäinen writes, the appearance of the term theosis is, at best, "rare in the biblical canon."[40] To evangelical ears, especially those come of age in the era of rationalistic modernism and steeped in the ethos of *sola scriptura*—"show me chapter and verse"—biblical exegesis, there seems an obvious disconnect between the above two statements. Theosis enjoys biblical support without the term itself even appearing in Scripture to any significant degree? "How," the Western modern might ask, "does *that* work?"

To understand this seeming contradiction, it helps to remind ourselves that both the Orthodox and the Catholic East sailed through the middle centuries of the second millennium largely beyond the reach of modernity and the rationalistic Enlightenment. While this difference in experience between East and West means many things, most relevant to

38. Bartos, *Deification*, 7.

39. Clendenin, *Eastern Orthodox*, 130.

40. Kärkkäinen, *One with God*, 123.

our discussion is that it certainly helps explain the different approaches to Scripture. Hence, while the Western believer exploring the credence of the Eastern doctrine of theosis might request of his Eastern Christian friend, "Show me chapter and verse," he might also note his Eastern friend's befuddlement at his query.

Alister McGrath notes the Christian West's historic embrace of rationalism, and its resultant rationalistic approaches to the Scriptures, in his *A Passion for Truth*. McGrath observes, with Hans Frei, that "the rise of rationalism led to a gradual rejection of the 'narrative' character of Scripture." He points out that, in contrast, for "precritical" (read, premodern) writers, "the interpretation of Scripture concerned 'an interpretation of stories and their meanings by weaving them together into a common narrative referring to a single history and its patterns of meaning.'"[41] McGrath lays the catalyst for this difference at the feet of the Enlightenment, proposing, "The Enlightenment, however, adopted a network of approaches to biblical interpretation which reflect the rationalism and anti-supernaturalism of the movement."[42]

Interestingly, in making these observations, McGrath is lobbying for a widening of the typical modernistic approaches to Scripture, which would allow for the reintroduction into evangelical exegesis of story and narrative. And while McGrath contrasts the legacy of modern evangelical approaches to Scripture with a "precritical" mindset and approach, he is really describing not simply a precritical but, at base, a pre*modern* approach to the Scriptures. Whether consciously or not, McGrath here is also offering a fairly accurate description of the Eastern approach to the Holy Scriptures. Indeed, for the Westerner seeking out a left-brained, rationalistic description of Eastern Christian exegetical methodology, such a search might prove somewhat frustrating. And perhaps even a bit humorous.

Clendenin, the Protestant scholar we met above, grapples with this phenomenon in his fine review of Eastern Orthodoxy, as he wrestles with the biblical basis for the doctrine of theosis.

> The Bible speaks extensively about theosis, according to the Orthodox tradition, and thus so must we. The two most direct texts are 2 Pet 1:4 and Ps 82:6 (John 10:34–35). If it be objected that these texts are taken out of context, or that finding the doctrine in

41. McGrath, *A Passion*, 105.

42. Ibid., 105.

an array of biblical texts is unconvincing, Orthodox theologians would care little.[43]

Clendenin expands on this thought by paraphrasing a quote of St. Maximus the Confessor from the Philokalia, the volumes that stand as the historic depository of Eastern Christian spirituality: "Sticking to the mere letter of Scripture proves only one's attachment to the senses and the flesh,"[44] insists the Confessor. Kärkkäinen echoes Clendenin here, almost wistfully remarking,

> Unfortunately, the Eastern Church has not been active in pursuing critical biblical studies on the concept of salvation, and if they have, they are not easily available to the theological guild. At this point, we simply lack reliable biblical studies. The Eastern theologians' supporting of their claim for the extensive biblical attestation of the idea of deification is more guided by apologetic concerns than theological accuracy.[45]

Perhaps Kärkkäinen has a point here. But presumably so does Clendenin. And if Kärkkäinen is frustrated by his perceived deficit on the part of his theological colleagues from the East, he might have also noted that in regards to this perceived deficit, his Eastern colleagues might, as Clendenin noted, "care little." In fairness to these Eastern colleagues, however, it should be quickly noted that their seeming lack of care on a point of intense Western concern is not petulant oversight or even sloppiness, but rather a matter of perspective. And tradition.

Bishop Kallistos Ware, perhaps the most enduring interpreter of Christian Orthodoxy to the West, deals with this characteristically Eastern approach to biblical study in his *The Orthodox Way*:

> As we read the Bible, we are all the time gathering information, wrestling with the sense of obscure sentences, comparing and analyzing. But this is secondary. The real purpose of Bible study is much more than this–to feed our love for Christ, to kindle our hearts into prayer, and to provide us with guidance in our personal life. The study of words should give place to an immediate dialog with the living Word himself.[46]

---

43. Clendenin, *Eastern Orthodox*, 125.

44. Ibid., 126.

45. Kärkkäinen, *One with God*, 123.

46. Ware, *Orthodox Way*, 148.

Granting these allowances, the Eastern scholar would nonetheless be able to provide a catalog of scriptural texts in defense of the doctrine of divinization. This catalog might not be limited to, but would certainly include the following:

1. On the formula of exchange: St. Paul's second letter to the church in Corinth (2 Cor 8:9) in which the Apostle writes, "For you know the grace of our Lord Jesus Christ, that though he was rich, yet for your sake he became poor so that you by his poverty might become rich."

2. Regarding the centrality of divine filiation—that is, our becoming "Sons of God"—found in numerous passages, including Gal 4:4–6; Rom 8:14–17 and 1 John 3:1, 2. "See what kind of love the Father has given to us that we should be called children of God; and so we are."

3. On our "becoming gods." (Ps 82:6).

4. On the possibility of our being "partakers of the divine nature," (2 Pet 1:4).

5. On our ultimately being transformed into the image of Christ, (Col 3:5–17).

6. On our redemption being understood as conformity to Christ and being transformed into his image (Rom 8:29; 2 Cor 3:18).

7. Our ongoing participation in Christ's death and resurrection as being catalytic to our ultimate deification (2 Cor 4:10–12; Phil 3:7–11; Rom 8:17).

8. The doctrine of participation as taught by the Fathers is related to their understanding of our redemption in Christ (Heb 2:14; Heb 6:4; Phil 2:1 and 1 Cor. 10:14–22).[47]

Theosis in the Narrative Arch of Divine *Oikonomia*

While Keating has helpfully provided us with this inventory of supportive biblical texts, he very interestingly concludes that, despite this line-up of scriptural support for the doctrine, far more important to the Eastern mind is

> the overarching biblical narrative for the doctrine of deification in Christ as the New Adam . . . In a sense, the doctrine of deification

47. Keating, *Deification and Grace*, 117.

is a biblically and doctrinally rich elaboration of what Paul states as our destiny in 1 Cor 15:49: "Just as we have borne the image of the man of dust, we shall also bear the image of the man of heaven."[48]

Keating's use of the term "overarching," with the image it suggests, is telling, and whether conscious and intended on his part we cannot know. But it is especially curious to discover the identical imagery used by the Orthodox scholar Andrew Louth, in his discussion of deification and its place in the divine economy. As we more closely consider both Keating's observation and Louth's point, we will begin to more clearly understand that what may initially appear, especially to Westerners, as an Eastern Christian lack of attention to biblical buttressing for theosis, is actually something more— much more.

In wrestling with the Eastern concept of divinization and its relation to the scriptural witness, Louth first locates deification as the ultimate end point, or *telos*, of human destiny. He then carefully places it within the totality of the divine economy:

> Deification, then, has to do with human destiny, a destiny that finds its fulfillment in a face-to-face encounter with God, an encounter in which God takes the initiative by meeting us in the Incarnation where we behold . . . "the glory of God in the face of Jesus Christ" (2 Cor 4:6). It is important for a full grasp of what this means to realize that deification is not to be equated with re-demption . . . But deification belongs to a broader conception of the divine *oikonomia*: deification is the fulfillment of creation, not just the rectification of the Fall.[49]

Louth then elaborates, suggesting that the best way to think of this divine economy, and the place and importance of humanity's divinization within it, is to "think in terms of an arch stretching from creation to deification, representing what is and remains God's intention: the creation of the cosmos that, through humankind, is destined to share in the divine life, to be deified."[50] He next suggests that

> the loss of the notion of deification leads to lack of awareness of the greater arch from creation to deification and thereby to con-centration on the lower arch, from Fall to redemption: it is, I think,

48. Ibid., 118.

49. Christensen and Wittung, *Partakers*, 34–35.

50. Ibid., 35.

not unfair to suggest that such a concentration on the lesser arch at the expense of the greater arch has been characteristic of much Western theology.[51]

Louth's concept of God's redemptive arch spanning from creation, not simply to the fall and the cross, but instead all the way across to include the deification of humanity and redemption available to the entire cosmos (to recall our reading of McKnight, above), is potentially and radically paradigm shifting. We have already seen, how McKnight advocates for evangelicals to recognize the cosmic implications of the full and robust *gospel of Jesus Christ*, juxtaposed to what he suggests has been the classical and narrow evangelical soterian focus on the Plan of Salvation (traditionally understood as yielding justification). Here McKnight, whether consciously or not, echoes Louth and other Orthodox theologians who understand the divine economy as an enterprise far greater than simply bringing about one's individual salvation. Indeed, these theologians regard the divine salvific economy, or narrative, as one that arches across the whole of human history and beyond. Louth summarizes this divine narrative, suggesting that in the doctrine of deification we can understand "that God created the world to unite it to himself; it preserves the sense that the purpose of creation is to achieve union with God."[52]

Hopefully, by now it has become more palatable to accept the notion that when we look to the East for biblical buttressing of the doctrine of deification, we should not expect to find an exegetical exercise parallel to what we might expect to find in the West. As we look to the East, instead of finding a rational, linear proof-texting support of theosis, we encounter a tapestry of narrative describing a divine economy in which the incarnation, the cross, and then the deification of humanity play a central role.

We see an example of this, for instance, in the *Life of Moses*, an iconic ancient classic on the soteriological pilgrimage of faithful believers, written in the fourth century by St. Gregory. In this work, Gregory certainly employs Scripture to support his understanding of the doctrine of the deification of humankind. And yet, in doing so, he is not primarily concerned with presenting an exegetical argument as would be expected of a Western scholar. Instead, the saint employs the life of Moses as a narrative and sort of ancient *Pilgrim's Progress* to convey the sweep or arch of salvific pilgrimage as played out in Moses' life. Here again, we encounter the Eastern

51. Ibid., 35.
52. Ibid., 36.

understanding of redemption as narrative, and not simply narrative on the individualistic level, but as a wide, sweeping, and cosmic narrative, encompassing the redemption and recapitulation of the entire cosmos. Writing in the introduction to the *Life*, scholars Malherbe and Ferguson explain that the work portrays "an incessant transformation into the likeness of God as man stretches with the divine infinity," and that "the theme that holds the whole work together, (is) the idea of eternal progress."[53] As St. Gregory told the story of Moses' life, his intent was not merely historical, but was, rather, to present a pastoral message through narrative. Once again, for St. Gregory, Moses' life was an icon, a beacon, lived to show the faithful who would follow him the way out of Egypt, through the desert, and into the Promised Land. Moses' pilgrimage, and our pilgrimage, is intended to be lived out toward the ultimate goal of our glorification and union with God. How great a salvation indeed!

As we have seen, through the early centuries of the first millennium, the Eastern theology of deification was being worked out in tandem with the development of a patristic, Orthodox Christology. As such, the doctrine of divinization was an assumptive posture of the early fathers. And as we have just surveyed, the Eastern faithful might quizzically greet a query from a modern, Western evangelical requesting a Western-style biblical defense of the doctrine of theosis. Nonetheless, these same faithful would regard the doctrine as a central and indispensable theme in the overarching cosmic narrative of God's intended redemption of humanity and, indeed, the entire cosmos.

In light of the above, we can summarize here that the doctrine of theosis by the midpoint of the first millennium, enjoyed both the assumptive support of the fathers and a central place in their evolving Trinitarian theology, specifically their Christology. We have also seen the weight of scriptural support brought to bear in support of the doctrine, even if it is "biblical support" of an Eastern rather than Western tradition.

Sola Scriptura vs. Church Tradition

Indeed, if in the West biblical "proof," especially when coupled with the support of noted and trusted theologians, can run the table, such is not the case in the Christian East. Along with these, before the Christian East (and Catholic West) embraces a doctrine, the doctrine must first clear

53. Gregory of Nyssa, *Life of Moses*, 12.

another hurdle—that being tradition, or rather, *Tradition*. While Western Protestantism has historically been suspicious of any qualifiers added to its doctrine of *sola scriptura*, this doctrine is unknown in the Christian East. Whether this Western doctrine will survive the advent of postmodernity and the epistemological spotlight it has shone on the question of what we can know, and how we know it, remains to be seen. Even so, while this important question has rightfully begun to be considered by serious evangelical scholars, it is not our central focus here. We will thus note it, but continue with our study of divinization, its credence, and what it could mean for the growing numbers of young and restless evangelicals.

While Western Christians might find the Eastern elevation of tradition strange, if not outright alarming, Orthodox Bishop Ware helps explain the importance and meaning of tradition in the theology of the ancient church. In making his point, Ware first establishes that "The Christian Church is a Scriptural Church: Orthodoxy believes this just as firmly, if not more firmly than Protestantism."[54] He then clarifies this by pointing out,

> The Bible is the supreme expression of God's revelation to man . . . But if Christians are People of the Book, the Bible is the Book of the People; it must not be regarded as something set up over the Church, but as something that lives and is understood within the Church (that is why one should not separate Scripture and Tradition).[55]

Ware continues, and further defines holy tradition as being the summation of "*living continuity* with the church of the ancient times."[56] He then summarizes these thoughts for the Eastern Christian faithful in general and Orthodox Christians in particular.

> It means the books of the Bible; it means the Creed; it means the decrees of the Ecumenical Councils and the writings of the Fathers; it means the Canons, the Service Books, the Holy Icons–in fact, the whole system of doctrine, Church government, worship, and art which Orthodoxy has articulated over the ages. The Orthodox Christian of today sees himself as heir and guardian to a great inheritance received from the past, and he believes that it is his duty to transmit this inheritance unimpaired to the future.[57]

54. Ware, *Orthodox Church*, 207.
55. Ibid., 207.
56. Ibid., 204.
57. Ibid., 204.

Finally, echoing St. John of Damascus of the seventh century, Ware emphasizes, "We do not change the everlasting boundaries which our fathers have set . . . But *we keep the Tradition, just as we received it.*"[58]

We can turn next to the noted church historian Jaroslav Pelikan, who suggests, "Drawing a sharp distinction between gospel and tradition had been a major plank in the platform of the Protestant Reformation."[59] Pelikan elaborates by suggesting that "the very antitraditionalism of the Reformation has itself become a tradition," and pays off the thought by proposing, "Protestants have, in this principle, nothing less than a full–blown tradition."[60] Some might suggest that Pelikan is overstating his case here, but assuming his points have merit, his ultimate conclusion is not without consequence; "And so the Bible was not 'the Bible only' after all,"[61] also merits serious consideration. Especially so, it would seem, in view of the shift from modernity to postmodernity, with the epistemological implications this shift entails. Finally, Pelikan makes a point that has direct implications for our consideration of the Eastern monks and their experience in prayer and journeys into divinization. Pelikan cites the Westerner Cardinal Newman, who said, "The ears of the common people are holier than are the hearts of the priests." What this suggests, proposes Pelikan, is that holy tradition is "a profoundly democratic concept, which did not trickle down from theologians, popes, and councils to the people, but filtered up from the faithful (who are the church)."[62]

The reason we have taken this seeming detour into the discussion of the place of tradition in the East versus West is that the development and working out of the doctrine of theosis in the Eastern church does not only reflect the theological model building of Eastern Christian theologians. Instead, as Pelikan suggests above, the doctrine of theosis itself was being explored early in the history of the faith, and lived out in the lives of the people—specifically, the monks of the desert. As such, this spiritual experience did not "trickle down from the theologians, popes and councils, but filtered up from the faithful." In this particular case, it took hundreds of years, from the initial exiles into the desert to a point in the fifteenth

58. Ibid., 204.

59. Pelikan, *Vindication of Tradition*, 9.

60. Ibid., 11.

61. Ibid., 11.

62. Ibid., 30.

century, for theosis, this "doctrine of the people," to be ultimately tested and proven in the councils of the Eastern church.

Theosis and the Witness of the Desert Monastics

Indeed, while the East is not noted for its speed in either exploring or embracing "new" theologies or their implications for the faith, nothing was not happening in these early centuries following the conversion of Constantine. During these centuries, the doctrine of divinization ceased being theory or "mere" theology, and began its graduation to a level of efficacious Christian formation. It was a particular class of men—though not exclusively men—who forced this evolution. These were the monks of the desert. Bishop Ware explains that with the conversion of Constantine, Christianity entered an era when "a martyrdom of blood no longer existed."[63] Though the existential threat of martyrdom was, by this time, no longer a reality, as the bishop explains, another threat arose in its place. This was that of the relatively fashionable and easy life into which Christianity might now degenerate, as it was now the official religion of empire. With this ease came the seduction, as Ware explains, of errantly "identifying the kingdom of God with an earthly kingdom." With their withdrawal from the world and flight to the desert, the monks "reminded Christians that the kingdom of God is not of this world."[64]

In effect, one might rightly conclude that in these monks we see an entire class of (primarily) men who concluded of the Christianity they had come to know and experience in the cities of the empire, "This isn't working." So in their own desperate yearning for authenticity, they fled the excesses of the city to embrace an austerity of life stripped of nearly everything excepting the pursuit of God. Ware elaborates on monasticism and the part it plays for all the Christian East: "Monasticism played a decisive part in the religious life of Byzantium, as it has done in that of all Orthodox countries. It has been rightly said that 'the best way to penetrate Orthodox spirituality is to enter it through Monasticism.'"[65]

The importance of this understanding and its relevance to our study is hinted at again by Ware, as he explains that in the Eastern Christian model

---

63. Ware, *Orthodox Church*, 45.

64. Ibid., 45.

65. Ibid.,, 46.

of spirituality "a monk's primary task is the life of prayer."[66] And pray they did. But, to reuse a phrase employed above, as the monks retreated to the desert to live their lives of prayer, working out their salvation within the greater narrative of cosmic redemption, *nothing* was not happening. In fact, a *lot* began happening, particularly in their prayers, while they disciplined themselves in formation to the image of Christ, as they understood it.

Through the centuries following Constantine, reports of what might be described as mystical experiences began filtering back into the cities from the desert hermits and monks. The Orthodox scholar John Meyendorff quotes St. Gregory Palamas, who was to come to the defense of the monks and their spirituality. The saint located these monastic spiritual experiences within the salvific arch, existent even in the Old Testament times:

> The doctrines that are today a common heritage, known by all and preached openly, were mysteries under the Mosaic law, and made accessible beforehand only to the vision of the prophets. So too the good things which the saints proclaim for the world to come, are the mysteries of the evangelical society, for the Spirit makes the saints worthy of the vision and they receive these good things and see them ahead of time, as first fruits.[67]

This thesis, that the monks experienced in their lives of prayer the "first fruits" of what is to come, is critical. As such, it means, as Meyendorff suggests, that the prayer lives of these monks and their lives of holiness are "thus essentially prophetic."[68] What we are seeing here, then, is Meyendorff placing the monastic experiences of divinization within the spectrum or arch of Louth's model. These monastic experiences, according to Meyendorff, as cited in his quote above, "were mysteries under the Mosaic Law." As such, the reported monastic experiences were "prophetic" in that they foretold of a blessed life, which, for most of us, will only become a fuller reality further across the redemptive arch of our own lives and into eternity. Even so, for these particular, prophetic monks, St. Gregory Palamas explained,

> Some of them have experienced true initiation—all those who have forsaken enjoyment of material possessing, human glory and corrupt bodily pleasure, choosing instead the evangelical life; those who have also intensified this abandonment of the world

66. Ibid., 46.

67. Meyendorff, *St. Gregory Palamas*, 95.

68. Ibid., 95.

by obedience to those who have already reached full manhood in Christ, free from all responsibility save for their own rigorous attention and pure prayer, reaching even God himself in a mystical and supra-intellectual union with him—they have been initiated into that which transcends the human mind . . . This deifying grace of God, according to the words of the godly Maximus, in speaking of Melchisedek, is uncreated, eternal, proceeding from the eternal God.[69]

These reports of monastic desert prayer experiences reached critical mass in the fourteenth century. The question of monastic spirituality thus became a flash point, with their spirituality coming under intense scrutiny from some in the church who vigorously questioned its orthodoxy. A drama of the monks in the dock unfolded, as their unique desert spirituality, with divinization as its centerpiece and goal, was called into question. Their successful defense, particularly by St. Gregory Palamas, and the ultimate vindication of monastic desert spirituality and its experience and understanding of stillness, quiet, and theosis, set the course of Eastern Christian spirituality—a course that remains to this day. This successful defense was so fundamental that Meyendorff describes it as "not as the triumph of a particular form of mysticism but of orthodoxy itself."[70]

Because the spiritual formation of these early monks, their spirituality, and its successful defense are key to our understanding of theosis, we will now review this fourteenth-century drama. As we do so, it will be fascinating to realize that the prayer lives and the question of spiritual formation of Christians worldwide have been directly affected by monastic disputes waged nearly seven hundred years ago.

Hesychasm and the Uncreated, Taboric Light

The term hesychasm began appearing in monastic literature as early as the fourth century.[71] Translated as "stillness," hesychasm was not simply monastic retirement from the world. Instead, the hesychastic monks, who fled what they considered the corruption of the cities of the empire, entered the silence of their desert cells as entering a workshop—in their case, a

69. Ibid., 95, 96.

70. Ibid., 9.

71. Meyendorff, *Byzantine Legacy*, 167.

workshop dedicated to the practice of unceasing prayer.[72] The prayer rule adopted by these desert monastics was a simple, rhythmic prayer that came to be called the Jesus Prayer. In its popular form, the Jesus Prayer is simply, "Lord Jesus Christ, Son of God, have mercy on me, a sinner." The hesychastic prayer rule often included the repetition of this prayer, at times accompanied by a particular bodily posture and rhythmic breathing.

St. Gregory of Sinai, of the fourteenth century, reintroduced hesychasm on the "Holy Mountain" of Mt. Athos, which, as a remote, peninsular outcropping into the Aegean Sea, had become the site of numerous monasteries and hermitical cells. These Athonite monks, practicing their hesychastic prayer rule, began reporting unique experiences resulting from their prayers, as noted above. They even reported encounters with what they claimed was the uncreated "Taboric Light."[73] This Light of Tabor was purported to be the same uncreated light of both the theophanies of the Old Testament and the transfiguration of the Lord in the New. It was, by the monks who had experienced this light, regarded as something other than a natural, "created, meteorological phenomenon . . . it was the light belonging by nature to God . . . existing outside created being. It appeared in the theophanies of the Old Testament as the glory of God."[74]

These monks, then, were essentially claiming to have experienced God, encountered as the fulfillment of their hesychastic prayers. They were, as Meyendorff explained above, claiming to have experienced "true initiation"—in this lifetime—"into the deifying grace of God." Metropolitan Hierotheos, a contemporary Orthodox scholar, explains that "the vision of the uncreated Light is the vision of the glory of God in the deified flesh of the Logos; the Second Person of the Holy Trinity . . . The vision of the uncreated Light constitutes the deification of man, because it comes about through the transformation of man."[75] In this understanding, the metropolitan enjoys the benefit of six hundred years of maturation of both church theology and tradition. But, for the Hesychasts claiming this encounter, it was a tougher sell, as it should have been, especially as they were claiming "direct and personal knowledge of God . . . through a mystical communion with Him."[76] And while this may have constituted an apt description of the

72. Ware, *Inner Kingdom*, 91.

73. Spidlik, *Spirituality of the Christian East*, 318.

74. Lossky, *Vision of God*, 161.

75. Hierotheos, *St. Gregory Palamas*, 301, 310.

76. Mantzaridis, *Deification of Man* 114.

monks' hesychastic experiences, to the extent of the abilities of language, not everyone agreed.

One who strongly disagreed was Barlaam, a Calabrian Greek monk and philosopher. Barlaam had heard reports of these monastic prayer experiences and was intrigued, so much so that he traveled to Thessaloniki to live among the Hesychasts and witness their alleged experiences. He was unimpressed, caustically reporting, "I have been initiated by them, in monstrosities and in absurd doctrines that a man with any intelligence . . . cannot lower himself to describe."[77] Barlaam's report ignited a firestorm, and it fell to St. Gregory Palamas, born in 1296, to come to the monks' defense.

Scholars have long wrestled with the multiple strands of this controversy, which included theological and anthropological issues, along with differing views of the nature of God and claims as to what can be known of him.[78] Numerous scholars conclude that this controversy is best described as the iconic conflict between the Christian world, East and West. George Dragas states, "Barlaam represents Western scholasticism, whereas the Monks and Gregory Palamas represent the tradition of the Fathers."[79] Others agree. "The humanists equated knowledge with erudition and a speculative exercise, termed by Barlaam as 'wisdom' . . . for Palamas the true message of the Gospel was spelt out not by the sharpness of logic . . . but through the mystical experiences of the hesychastic saints."[80]

In typical Byzantine fashion, the conflict ultimately embroiled not only the theologians, bishops, and monks, but also the emperor, empress and multiple church councils. After three such councils, St. Gregory, hesychasm, the monks, and their reported encounters with the uncreated Taboric Light were vindicated.[81] Censured, Barlaam retreated to the Latin West, which was itself gradually evolving away from the *zeitgeist* of the more mystical East, toward a rationalism that would come to full flower in the Enlightenment.

Though this process—the monastic flight to the desert, followed by the development of their hesychastic prayer rule and reports of direct encounter with the divine—evolved over hundreds of years, its validation became a key component of Eastern Christian tradition. Again, as Pelikan

77. Meyendorff, *St. Gregory Palamas*, 89.

78. Meyendorff, *Byzantine Legacy*, 173–74.

79. Dragas, "Synods and Theology," 633–34.

80. Costache, "Experiencing the Divine Life," 3.

81. Dragas, "Synods and Theology," 633–34.

writes, this monastic experience of deification "did not trickle down from theologians, popes, and councils to the people, but filtered up from the faithful (who are the church)."[82]

Desert Monastics and Postmodern Millennials

At this point, we should remind ourselves why we are concerned at all with the prayer lives and especially the spiritual experiences of Eastern, hesychastic monks. Put bluntly, perhaps the crisis in contemporary evangelicalism demands it. If, as it seems they are, legions of young evangelicals are fleeing the churches of their youth for a reason parallel to that for which the Eastern monks fled the cities to the desert—because "It's not working for me"—then perhaps the monks' stories and experiences of encounters with God are especially relevant to us today. In his *Ancient-Future Faith*, Robert Webber makes a related point. He observes that postmodernity has revived an appreciation of both symbol and mystery,[83] and, in illustration, he shares the fears of a Presbyterian friend: "If we don't restore the Eucharist to its rightful place in our churches, we are going to lose many of our children to the liturgical churches."[84]

At this point, we may recall the eerie and plaintive synopsis of the deservedly admired Dallas Willard, who concluded that while "the evangelical form of Christian faith has achieved remarkable acceptance and prominence in recent decades . . . we have not done well in four critical areas."[85] Willard then lists these four, two of which are uniquely related to our study, and particularly telling: "We have not figured out," suggests Willard, "what the spiritual life is really like," nor have we "dealt successfully with the challenge of transforming our characters into routine Christlikeness."[86]

Hopefully, it is not unfair to "translate" Willard's synopsis by suggesting that—to borrow from Louth's model of the arch of salvation—we have in some measure, at least, failed to move very far along beneath that arch toward our ultimate destiny of union with God. If this is at all true, perhaps the cause is not simply recalcitrance, or sin. Possibly it is something else. Perhaps it is what McKnight is pushing for as he attempts to expand our

---

82. Pelikan, *Vindication of Tradition*, 30.
83. Webber, *Ancient-Future Faith*, 109.
84. Ibid., 110.
85. Tomlinson, *Post Evangelical*, 12.
86. Ibid., 12.

understanding of salvation from the Plan of Salvation, to an embrace of the robust, full-orbed, cosmos-redeeming *gospel of King Jesus*. Perhaps it is simply that we have *forgotten*. Like the Hebrews who had forgotten the fullness of who they were, and who their God was, until they rediscovered the holy scrolls hidden within the walls of the temple, it may be needful for us to recall and rediscover the fullness of our ancient faith, and also who we are—and who our God is.

Veli-Matti Kärkkäinen makes an observation well worth our consideration: "Any religion that wants to redeem its promises should give an answer to the most profound question of human life, namely, what is the way back to God, to live with God, to live in God and share in the divine?" He follows up by answering his own question. "Christian theology from the beginning has offered an answer to the world and its followers in the form of the doctrine of deification and/or union with God."[87]

At base is the fundamental question, "What *is* salvation?" As we have seen, evangelicalism was birthed and grew alongside its siblings, modernity and the Enlightenment. For a time, this familial association and pedigree served the cause of evangelicalism well. "Evangelicalism," recalling from Dallas Willard, "has achieved remarkable acceptance and prominence in recent decades."

Now, however, evangelicalism has reached its own inflection point. Varied and sincere voices are calling for a buffet of possible new directions and "solutions" to perceived challenges. For some, if evangelicalism is to survive, everything must change. For others, such a radical prescription might well save the brand while killing the patient. Others may even suggest that at this late date, a defensive circling of the wagons is all that can be hoped for.

Theosis and the Problem of Human Yearning

If Kärkkäinen's analysis is correct in saying that the most profound yearning of human life is to find a "way back to God, to live with God, to live in God and share in the divine," then any hopes evangelical leaders might have of answering their youths' yearnings (and staunching their exodus from the churches) with still more programs or stylistic adjustments are doomed to failure. Instead, I would propose that a true answer to this yearning lies in looking back. Back to the monks of the East whose prayer rules culminated

87. Kärkkäinen, *One with God*, 1.

in their articulate silences and, at times, less-than-articulate attempts to explain what they had seen and experienced.

While the lives and testimonies of these monks can sound foreign and exotic to our Western ears, they deserve a listen, nonetheless. As we have seen, their lives and their spirituality enjoy the testimony and validation of the fathers of the church. They thus enjoy a place in the soteriological narrative of Christendom—the overarching gospel story of our redemption. They enjoy as well the witness and support of Scripture, as well as a central place in the tradition of our church—especially relevant when we understand church tradition as the movement of the Holy Spirit through the ages. Finally, we must understand that these monastics who fled to the desert and claimed to have entered the silence, meeting God himself, are not solely monastics and holy men and women of the *Eastern* church. If we are in Christ, they are all of our monks, and holy fathers and holy mothers to us all. And if there is veracity to their experience and their claims—and a critical mass of the Christian church and witness believes there is—then, yes, this *could* change everything. Indeed, as Meyendorff has indicated, the monks and their experiences of God in theosis are prophetic. That is, their lives and experiences point forward, anticipating the far reaches of the arch of salvation.

Theosis, Sanctification, and Salvation

"But," some might protest, "what you're really (only) talking about is sanctification." There is much to be said about and for the Reformation concept of sanctification. Even so, as Finlan and Kharlamov suggest in their study of theosis, "simply replacing theosis with sanctification is an attempt to supplant Patristic theology with standard Reformation language."[88] Is this a defensive overstatement? I think not. A growing number of sympathetic Protestant scholars are looking to the spirituality of the Christian East and exploring there the doctrine of theosis, or union with God. We have already heard from some, including Clark Pinnock and Daniel Clendenin, and there are others, such as Tuomo Mannermaa of the "New Finnish School." Just as interesting are the scholarly efforts of some to mine the theology of the Reformers themselves to discover there a nascent embrace of and pointing to the doctrine of theosis. Daniel Keating suggests that "aspects of deification can also be found in the writings of key Protestant Reformers

88. Finlan and Kharlamov, *Theosis*, 5.

and theologians (Martin Luther, John Calvin, John Wesley), and many in the Protestant world are calling for a retrieval of the idea of salvation as deification."[89] Indeed, the close of the twentieth century witnessed the "dramatic change in the attitude of Western theologians towards the concept of deification."[90] According to Paul Gavrilyuk, the Orthodox scholar,

> A growing number of Western theologians—Augustine, Augustine of Canterbury, Thomas Aquinas, John of the Cross, Martin Luther, John Calvin . . . even the Radical Reformers and so on—have now been claimed to have taught a version of deification.[91]

While some might view these developments as a sign of possible rapprochement between the Christian East and West, others caution that until some definitional heavy lifting has been done, expectations should remain muted. While theologians of the New Finnish School have begun exploring common ground between the Reformed West and the Christian East,[92] others, such as their countryman Veli-Matti Kärkkäinen, caution that while deification, as understood in the East, may parallel the Western understanding of salvation, definitional precision is critical, especially since in the East,

> Salvation, then, is not primarily viewed as liberation from sin even though that is not a matter of indifference, but rather as a return to life immortal and the re-shaping of the human being into the image of her creator . . . Eastern theology takes the New Testament term soteria (salvation) in its biblical sense, which goes beyond terms such as "redemption," "reconciliation," "justification," and the like to encompass the wholeness of new life under God.[93]

But it isn't just the Christian East that paints the picture of Christian salvation in such large and sweeping strokes. Indeed, the well-known Western Catholic monk Thomas Merton also wrote,

> Finally, however, there will come a mystical transformation in which we will be perfectly conformed to the likeness of Christ. The Second Adam will live entirely in us. We will be "the New Man" who is, in fact, One Man—the One Christ, Head and Members.[94]

89. Keating, *Deification and Grace*, 119.
90. Gavrilyuk, "Retrieval of Deification," 648.
91. Ibid., 648.
92. Braaten and Jenson, *Union with Christ*, 25.
93. Kärkkäinen, *One with God*, 23.
94. Merton, *New Man*, 158.

For classical evangelicalism to survive and thrive into the future—especially a future featuring the above-described journey into postmodernity—courage will be required. And humility. It will require the courage to recognize that the overall cultural endorsement along with the modernistic, rationalistic scaffolding—twin supports evangelicalism has always enjoyed—have both largely fallen away. Increasingly, evangelicals will need to face a future without the support of either/or finality and certainty. Their youths have already entered that future, and the jury is still out on what they will make of it. Likewise, humility will be needed to admit that grafting management techniques onto their local churches will not suffice in facing this challenge. Nor will programmatic sophistication or dizzying production values. The scaffolding has fallen and there is no building it back up again. Will evangelicalism stand?

"Come Up Here": The Call for a New Mysticism

Instead, what must be recognized is that the world was never, really, wholly as we moderns imagined or even measured it out to be. At the core of the cosmos lies not an elegant equation or mathematical grand unification theory holding all the pieces together. Indeed, what lies resident at the core of the cosmos, pulsating and vivifying all that is, is the communion of Trinitarian love. God himself. Amazingly, this love beckons to any and all who will courageously make the journey to "Come up here."

So move ahead we must. We cannot go back. Evangelical youths are protesting with their feet and their voices that the status quo simply "isn't working." They are protesting that they will no longer tolerate an evangelicalism that forces them rightward in so many ways—politically, socially, philosophically, culturally, ecclesiastically, and theologically. It would be a tragedy if they ultimately sought settlement of their grievances by simply and reflexively pushing leftward, to wherever that might lead, to offset their sense of having been shoved right. This reflexive response would likely occasion that their own children will likewise compensate by pushing back again toward the center, away from their millennial parents. And so the generational pendulum swings. What if, instead of pushing left to compensate a rightward legacy, we opt to instead take steps *up*—fledgling steps up toward and into the communal mystery of life in and with the Holy Trinity?

Dr. O correctly perceived that denying the hegemony of modernity's philosophical paradigm would lead to mysticism in some form. The

Orthodox theologian Vladimir Lossky recognizes this as well, but assures us,

> We must live the dogma expressing a revealed truth, which appears to us as an unfathomable mystery, in such a fashion that instead of assimilating the mystery to our mode of understanding, we should, on the contrary, look for a profound change, an inner transformation of spirit, enabling us to experience it mystically. Far from being mutually opposed, theology and mysticism support and complete each other.[95]

So, yes, there is mystery. But there always *was*. Even our best-reasoned and rationally constructed theological systems, inevitably, had mystery resident at their core. Again, as Lossky writes, in the early pages of his book on the theology of the Eastern church, "Mysticism is accordingly treated in the present work as the perfecting and crown of all theology: as theology *par excellence.*"[96]

The King Jesus Gospel:
Where Myth and History Have Met and Fused

Looking to this exciting but undetermined future, full of opportunity and promise, one is reminded of the conversation between the children and Mr. and Mrs. Beaver in C. S. Lewis' *The Lion, The Witch and the Wardrobe*, as the children anticipate meeting Aslan.

> "But we shall see him?" asked Susan.
> "Why, Daughter of Eve, that's what I brought you here for. I'm to lead you where you shall meet him," said Mr. Beaver.
> "Is—is he a man?" asked Lucy.
> "Aslan a man!" said Mr. Beaver sternly. "Certainly not. I tell you he is the King of the wood and the son of the great Emperor-Beyond-the-Sea. Don't you know who is the King of Beasts? Aslan is a lion—*the* Lion, the great Lion."
> "Ooh!" said Susan, "I'd thought he was a man. Is he—quite safe? I shall feel rather nervous about meeting a lion."
> "That you will, dearie, and no mistake," said Mrs. Beaver, "if there's anyone who can appear before Aslan without their knees knocking, they're either braver than most or else just silly."

95. Lossky, *Mystical Theology*, 9.
96. Ibid., 9.

"Then he isn't safe? said Lucy.

"Safe?" said Mr. Beaver. "Don't you hear what Mrs. Beaver tells you? Who said anything about safe? 'Course he isn't safe. But he's good. He's the King, I tell you."

"I'm longing to see him," said Peter, "even if I do feel frightened when it comes to the point."[97]

Truly, not *safe*, but truly *good*. And, in our best moments, we too long to see him. Indeed, this is what we have been brought here for: that we "may be filled with all the fullness of God" (Eph 3:19).

97. Lewis, *Lion*, 75–76.

Bibliography

Allen, Diogenes. *Christian Belief in a Postmodern World: The Full Wealth of Conviction.* Louisville: Westminster/John Knox, 1989.

Anderson, Walter T. *Reality Isn't What It Used to Be: Theatrical Politics, Ready-to-Wear Religion, Global Myths, Primitive Chic, and Other Wonders of the Postmodern World.* San Francisco: HarperSanFrancisco, 1990.

Bainton, Roland H. *Christendom.* Vol. 2. New York: Harper, 1964.

Baker, Hunter. *The End of Secularism.* Wheaton: Crossway, 2009.

Barbour, Ian G. *Issues in Science and Religion.* Englewood Cliffs, NJ: Prentice-Hall, 1966.

Barna, George. *Revolution.* Wheaton: Tyndale Momentum, 2012.

Bartos, Emil. *Deification in Eastern Orthodox Theology: An Evaluation and Critique of the Theology of Dumitru Stăniloae.* Waynesboro, GA: Paternoster, 1999.

Barzun, Jacques. *From Dawn to Decadence: 500 Years of Western Cultural Life.* New York: Harper Collins, 2000.

Bass, Diana Butler. *Christianity after Religion: The End of Church and the Birth of a New Spiritual Awakening.* New York: HarperOne, 2012.

Bebbington, D. B. "Evangelical Christianity and the Enlightenment." *Crux* 25 (1989) 30.

Berger, Peter L. *The Desecularization of the World: Resurgent Religion and World Politics.* Washington, DC: Ethics and Public Policy Center, 1999.

———. *The Homeless Mind: Modernization and Consciousness.* New York: Random House, 1973.

———. *The Noise of Solemn Assemblies: Christian Commitment and the Religious Establishment in America..* Garden City, NY: Doubleday, 1961.

———. *A Rumor of Angels: Modern Society and the Rediscovery of the Supernatural.* Garden City, NY: Doubleday, 1969.

Berger, Peter L., and Thomas Luckmann. *The Social Construction of Reality: A Treatise in the Sociology of Knowledge.* Garden City, NY: Doubleday, 1967.

Berman, Morris. *The Reenchantment of the World.* Ithaca, NY: Cornell University Press, 1981.

Bohm, David. *On Creativity.* New York: Routledge, 1996.

Braaten, Carl E., and Robert W. Jenson, eds. *Union with Christ: The New Finnish Interpretation of Luther.* Grand Rapids: Eerdmans, 1998.

Brown, Colin. *Christianity & Western Thought: A History of Philosophers, Ideas & Movements.* Vol. 1. Downers Grove, IL: InterVarsity, 1990.

Brown, Laurence Binet, Bernard C. Farr, and R. Joseph. Hoffmann. *Modern Spiritualities: An Inquiry.* Amherst, NY: Prometheus, 1997.

Brown, Robert McAfee. *The Spirit of Protestantism.* New York: Oxford University Press, 1961.

Capra, Fritjof. *The Tao of Physics: An Exploration of the Parallels between Modern Physics and Eastern Mysticism.* Boston: Shambhala, 2000.

———. *The Turning Point: Science, Society, and the Rising Culture.* Toronto: Bantam, 1983.

Carlson, Kent, and Mike Lueken. *Renovation of the Church: What Happens When a Seeker Church Discovers Spiritual Formation.* Downers Grove, IL: InterVarsity, 2011.

Carson, D. A. *Becoming Conversant with the Emerging Church: Understanding a Movement and Its Implications.* Grand Rapids: Zondervan, 2005.

Castaneda, Carlos. *The Teachings of Don Juan: A Yaqui Way of Knowledge.* New York: Pocket Books, 1968.

Chelsen, Paul O. "An Examination of Internet Pornography Usage among Male Students at Evangelical Christian Colleges." PhD diss., Loyola University, 2011.

Christensen, Michael J., and Jeffery A. Wittung, eds. *Partakers of the Divine Nature: The History and Development of Deification in the Christian Traditions.* Madison, NJ: Fairleigh Dickinson University Press, 2007.

Clendenin, Daniel B. *Eastern Orthodox Christianity: A Western Perspective.* Grand Rapids: Baker, 1994.

Copleston, Frederick. *A History of Philosophy.* Vol. 3. New York: Image, 1993.

———. *A History of Philosophy.* Vols. 4, 5, and 6. New York: Image, 1985.

Costache, Doru. "Experiencing the Divine Life: Levels of Participation in St. Gregory Palamas' *On The Divine and Deifying Participation.*" *Phronema* 26 (2011) 9–25.

Cox, Harvey. *The Future of Faith.* New York: HarperOne, 2009.

Davis, Justin L., R. Greg Bell, and G. Tyge Payne. "Stale in the Pulpit? Leader Tenure and the Relationship between Market Growth Strategy and Church Performance." *International Journal of Nonprofit and Voluntary Sector Marketing* 15 (2010) 352–68.

DeYoung, Kevin, and Ted Kluck. *Why We're Not Emergent: By Two Guys Who Should Be.* Chicago: Moody, 2008.

Dockery, David S. *The Challenge of Postmodernism: An Evangelical Engagement.* Grand Rapids: Baker Academic, 2001.

Downing, David C. *Into the Region of Awe: Mysticism in C. S. Lewis.* Downers Grove, IL: InterVarsity, 2005.

Dragas, George D. "Synods and Theology Connected with Hesychasm: The Synodical Procedure Followed in the Hesychastic Disputes." *Greek Orthodox Theological Review* 45 (2000) 631–46.

Drane, John. *What Is the New Age Still Saying to the Church?* New York: Harper Collins, 1991.

Dreyer, Elizabeth A. "How to Remain Faithful in a Consuming Culture and Is New Age Spirituality All That New?" *Religious Studies Review* 34 (2008) 1–8.

Ellwood, Robert S. *The Sixties Spiritual Awakening: American Religion Moving from Modern to Postmodern.* New Brunswick, NJ: Rutgers University Press, 1994.

Erickson, Millard J. *Postmodernizing the Faith: Evangelical Responses to the Challenge of Postmodernism.* Grand Rapids: Baker, 1998.

Evans, Rachel Held. "15 Reasons I Left Church." March 20, 2012. http://rachelheldevans.com/blog/15-reasons-i-left-church.

Farrell, Justin. "The Young and the Restless? The Liberalization of Young Evangelicals." *Journal for the Scientific Study of Religion* 50 (2011) 525.

Ferguson, Marilyn. *The Aquarian Conspiracy: Personal and Social Transformation in the 1980s.* Los Angeles: J. P. Tarcher, 1980.

Finlan, Stephen, and Vladimir Kharlamov. *Theōsis: Deification in Christian Theology.* Eugene, OR: Pickwick, 2006.

Fowler, Timothy. "As minority, US Protestants need to change stance, says professor." *Ecumenical News*, June 1, 2013. http://www.ecumenicalnews.com/article/as-minority-us-protestants-need-to-change-stance-says-professor/22243.htm.

Freeman, Stephen. "Words from St. Isaac of Syria." *Glory to God for All Things*, November 1, 2006. http://glory2godforallthings.com/2006/11/01/words-from-st-isaac-of-syria/.

Fuller, Edmund. *Myth, Allegory, and Gospel; an Interpretation of J. R. R. Tolkien, C. S. Lewis, G. K. Chesterton and Charles Williams.* Minneapolis: Bethany Fellowship, 1974.

Gavrilyuk, Paul L. "The Retrieval of Deification: How a Once-Despised Archaism Became an Ecumenical Desideratum." *Modern Theology* 25 (2009) 647–59.

Gibbs, Eddie, and Ryan K. Bolger. *Emerging Churches: Creating Christian Community in Postmodern Cultures.* Grand Rapids: Baker Academic, 2005.

Gregory of Nyssa. *The Life of Moses.* Translated by Abraham J. Malherbe and Everett Ferguson. New York: Paulist, 1978.

Grenz, Stanley J. *A Primer on Postmodernism.* Grand Rapids: Eerdmans, 1996.

———. *The Social God and the Relational Self: A Trinitarian Theology of the Imago Dei.* Louisville: Westminster John Knox, 2001.

Grenz, Stanley J., and John R. Franke. *Beyond Foundationalism: Shaping Theology in a Postmodern Context.* Louisville: Westminster John Knox, 2001.

Groothuis, Douglas R. *Truth Decay: Defending Christianity Against the Challenges of Postmodernism.* Downers Grove, IL: InterVarsity, 2000.

Gross, Jules. *The Divinization of the Christian according to the Greek Fathers.* Anaheim, CA: A & C, 2002.

Guardini, Romano. *The End of the Modern World.* Rev. ed. Wilmington, DE: ISI, 2001.

Harper, Kenneth C. "Francis A. Schaeffer: An Evaluation." *Biblioteca Sacra* 133 (1976) 130–42.

Haykin, Michael A. G., and Kenneth J. Stewart, eds. *The Advent of Evangelicalism: Exploring Historical Continuities.* Nashville: B & H Academic, 2008.

Hayward, John. "A General Model of Church Growth and Decline." *Journal of Mathematical Sociology* 29 (2005) 177–207.

Henry, Carl F. H. *Frontiers in Modern Theology.* Chicago: Moody, 1964.

Herrick, James A. *The Making of the New Spirituality: The Eclipse of the Western Religious Tradition.* Downers Grove, IL: InterVarsity, 2003.

Hesse, Hermann. *The Journey to the East.* Translated by Hilda Rosner. New York: Picador, 2003.

———. *Siddhartha.* Boston: Shambhala, 2005.

Hicks, Stephen Ronald Craig. *Explaining Postmodernism: Skepticism and Socialism from Rousseau to Foucault.* Phoenix: Scholargy, 2004.

Hinson, E. Glenn. *Spirituality in Ecumenical Perspective.* Louisville: Westminster/John Knox, 1993.

Hodder, Jacqueline. "Spirituality and Well-Being: 'New Age" and 'Evangelical' Spiritual Expressions among Young People and Their Implications for Well-Being." *International Journal of Children's Spirituality* 14 (2009) 197–212.

Holmes, Arthur F. *Christian Philosophy in the 20th Century.* Nutley: Craig, 1969.

Hunter, James Davison. *Evangelicalism: The Coming Generation.* Chicago: University of Chicago, 1987.

Hunter, Todd D. *Christianity beyond Belief: Following Jesus for the Sake of Others.* Downers Grove, IL: InterVarsity, 2009.

Huxley, Aldous. *The Doors of Perception: Heaven and Hell.* New York: Harper Colophon, 1963.

Inge, William R. *The Platonic Traditions in English Religious Thought.* New York: Longmans, Green, 1926.

jbernal. "Is Philosophy a Footnote to Plato?" *Philosophy Lounge,* December 19, 2010. http://www.philosophylounge.com/philosophy-footnote-plato/.

Johnson, Paul. *The Birth of the Modern: World Society, 1815–1830.* New York: HarperCollins, 1991.

———. *A History of Christianity.* New York: Atheneum, 1976.

———. *Modern Times: The World from the Twenties to the Eighties.* New York: Harper & Row, 1983.

Jones, Cheslyn, Geoffery Wainwright, and Edward Yarnold, eds. *The Study of Spirituality.* New York: Oxford University Press, 1986.

Jones, L. Gregory, and James Joseph Buckley. *Spirituality and Social Embodiment.* Oxford: Blackwell, 1997.

Jones, Robert P., Daniel Cox, Juhem Navarro-Rivera, E. J. Dionne Jr., and William A. Galston. "Do Americans Believe Capitalism & Government Are Working?" http://www.brookings.edu/research/reports/2013/07/18-economic-values-survey-capitalism-government-prri-dionne-galston.

Karlgaard, Rich. "Peter Drucker on Leadership." www.ceoproject.com/pdf/Articles/Drucker on leadership.pdf.

Kavanaugh, John F. *Following Christ in a Consumer Society: The Spirituality of Cultural Resistance.* Maryknoll, NY: Orbis, 1981.

Keating, Daniel A. *Deification and Grace.* Naples, FL: Sapientia, 2007.

Kelsey, Morton T. *The Other Side of Silence: A Guide to Christian Meditation.* New York: Paulist, 1976.

Kerouac, Jack. *The Dharma Bums.* New York: Signet, 1958.

Kharlamov, Vladimir, ed. *Theōsis: Deification in Christian Theology.* Eugene, OR: Pickwick, 2011.

Kinnaman, David, and Aly Hawkins. *You Lost Me: Why Young Christians Are Leaving Church—and Rethinking Faith.* Grand Rapids: Baker, 2011.

Kinnaman, David, and Gabe Lyons. *Unchristian: What a New Generation Really Thinks about Christianity—and Why It Matters.* Grand Rapids: Baker, 2007.

Kärkkäinen, Veli–Matti. *One with God: Salvation as Deification and Justification.* Collegeville, MN: Liturgical, 2004.

Kreeft, Peter, *The Platonic Tradition: Understanding Plato's Impact through the Ages.* Audiobook on CD–ROM, disc 1. Prince Frederick, MD: Recorded Books, 2012.

Lattin, Don. *The Harvard Psychedelic Club: How Timothy Leary, Ram Dass, Huston Smith, and Andrew Weil Killed the Fifties and Ushered in a New Age for America.* New York: HarperOne, 2010.

Latourette, Kenneth Scott. *A History of Christianity*. Vols. 1 and 2. New York: Harper & Row, 1975.

Lewis, C. S. *The Lion, the Witch and the Wardrobe*. New York: Collier, 1976.

Little, Paul E. *Know Why You Believe*. Downers Grove, IL: InterVarsity, 1975.

Lossky, Vladimir. *The Mystical Theology of the Eastern Church*. Crestwood, NY: St. Vladimir's Seminary Press, 1976.

———. Vladimir. *The Vision of God*. Crestwood, NY: St. Vladimir's Seminary Press, 1983.

Lyons, Gabe. *The Next Christians: The Good News about the End of Christian America*. New York: Doubleday, 2010.

Lyotard, Jean-François. *The Postmodern Condition: A Report on Knowledge*. Minneapolis: University of Minnesota, 1993.

Maddox, Marion. "'In the Goofy Parking Lot': Growth Churches as a Novel Religious Form for Late Capitalism." *Social Compass* 59 (2012) 146–58.

Marty, Martin. "The Years of the Evangelicals." *The Christian Century*, February 15, 1989. 171–74.

Mantzaridēs, Geōrgios I. *The Deification of Man: St. Gregory Palamas and the Orthodox Tradition*. Crestwood, NY: St. Vladimir's Seminary Press, 1984.

Marsden, George M. *Evangelicalism and Modern America*. Grand Rapids: Eerdmans, 1984.

———. *Fundamentalism and American Culture: The Shaping of Twentieth Century Evangelicalism, 1870–1925*. 2nd ed. New York: Oxford University Press, 2006.

———. "Fundamentalism as an American Phenomenon: A Comparison with English Evangelicalism." *Church History* 46 (1977) 215–32.

———. *Understanding Fundamentalism and Evangelicalism*. Grand Rapids: Eerdmans, 1991.

Mascall, E. L. *The Secularization of Christianity: An Analysis and a Critique*. New York: Holt, Rinehart, and Winston, 1966.

Maximus, Confessor, Saint. *On the Cosmic Mystery of Jesus Christ: Selected Writings from St. Maximus the Confessor*. Translated by Paul M. Blowers and Robert Louis Wilken. Crestwood, NY: St. Vladimir's Seminary Press, 2003.

May, Henry F. *The Enlightenment in America*. New York: Oxford University Press, 1976.

McDowell, Josh. *The New Evidence that Demands a Verdict*. Nashville: T. Nelson, 1999.

McGrath, Alister E. *Evangelicalism & the Future of Christianity*. Downers Grove, IL: InterVarsity, 1995.

———. *A Passion for Truth: The Intellectual Coherence of Evangelicalism*. Downers Grove, IL: InterVarsity, 1996.

McKnight, Scot *The King Jesus Gospel: The Original Good News Revisited*. Grand Rapids: Zondervan, 2011.

McKnight, Scot, Peter Rollins, Kevin Corcoran, and Jason Clark. *Church in the Present Tense: A Candid Look at What's Emerging*. Grand Rapids: Brazos, 2011.

McLaren, Brian D. *Everything Must Change: Jesus, Global Crises, and a Revolution of Hope*. Nashville: T. Nelson, 2007.

———. *A Generous Orthodoxy*. Grand Rapids: Zondervan, 2004.

———. *The Story We Find Ourselves In: Further Adventures of a New Kind of Christian*. San Francisco: Jossey-Bass, 2003.

McNeal, Reggie. *Missional Communities: The Rise of the Post-Congregational Church*. San Francisco: Jossey-Bass, 2011.

Merton, Thomas. *The New Man*. New York: Farrar, Straus & Cudahy, 1961.

Hierotheos, Metropolitan of Nafpaktos. *St. Gregory Palamas as a Hagiorite*. Translated by Esther Williams. Levadia, Greece: Birth of the Theotokos Monastery, 1997.

Meyendorff, John. *The Byzantine Legacy in the Orthodox Church*. Crestwood, NY: St. Vladimir's Seminary Press, 1982.

———. *St. Gregory Palamas and Orthodox Spirituality*. Crestwood, NY: St. Vladimir's Seminary Press, 1974.

Meyendorff, John, and Robert Tobias. *Salvation in Christ: A Lutheran-Orthodox Dialogue*. Minneapolis: Augsburg, 1992.

Middleton, J. Richard, and Brian J. Walsh. *Truth Is Stranger than It Used to Be: Biblical Faith in a Postmodern Age*. Downers Grove, IL: InterVarsity, 1995.

Nellas, Panayiotis. *Deification in Christ: Orthodox Perspectives on the Nature of the Human Person*. Crestwood, NY: St. Vladimir's Seminary Press, 1987.

Noll, Mark A. *The Scandal of the Evangelical Mind*. Grand Rapids: Eerdmans, 1994.

Noll, Mark, Cornelius Plantinga Jr., and David Wells. "The Intellectual Failure of American Evangelicals." *Theology Today* 51 (1995) 495–507.

Oden, Thomas C. *After Modernity . . . What?: Agenda for Theology*. Grand Rapids: Zondervan, 1992.

———. *The Rebirth of Orthodoxy: Signs of New Life in Christianity*. San Francisco: HarperSanFrancisco, 2003.

———. *Systematic Theology*. Vol. 3, *Life in the Spirit*. Peabody, MA: Hendrickson, 2008.

Olson, Roger E. *Reformed and Always Reforming: The Postconservative Approach to Evangelical Theology*. Grand Rapids: Baker Academic, 2007.

Peat, F. David. *Infinite Potential: The Life and Times of David Bohm*. Reading, MA: Helix, 1997.

Pelikan, Jaroslav. *The Vindication of Tradition*. New Haven, CT: Yale University Press, 1984.

Pew Forum on Religion & Public Life. "U.S. Religious Landscape Survey: Religious Beliefs and Practices: Diverse and Politically Relevant." June 2008. http://www.pewforum. org/files/2008/06/report2-religious-landscape-study-full.pdf.

Pinnock, Clark H. *Flame of Love: A Theology of the Holy Spirit*. Downers Grove, IL: InterVarsity, 1996.

Pirsig, Robert M. *Zen and the Art of Motorcycle Maintenance: An Inquiry into Values*. New York: Morrow, 1974.

Plato. "Plato's Similes of the Cave and the Divided Line." http://cw.routledge.com/ testbooks/alevelphilosophy/data/A2/Plato/PlatoSimilesLineCave.pdf.

Postman, Neil. *Technopoly: The Surrender of Culture to Technology*. New York: Vintage, 1993.

Purtill, Richard L. *Reasons to Believe*. Grand Rapids: Eerdmans, 1974.

Randall, Ian M. "Outgrowing Combative Boundary-Setting: Billy Graham, Evangelism and Fundamentalism." *Evangelical Review of Theology* 34 (2010) 103–18.

Rollins, Peter. *How (Not) to Speak of God*. Brewster, MA: Paraclete, 2006.

Roszak, Theodore. *The Making of a Counter Culture: Reflections on the Technocratic Society and Its Youthful Opposition*. Berkeley: University of California Press, 1995.

Russell, Bertrand. *A History of Western Philosophy*. New York: Simon and Schuster, 1972.

Russell, Norman. *The Doctrine of Deification in the Greek Patristic Tradition*. Oxford: Oxford University Press, 2006.

———. *Fellow Workers with God: Orthodox Thinking on Theosis*. Crestwood, NY: St. Vladimir's Seminary Press, 2009.

Schaeffer, Francis A. *The Church at the End of the 20th Century*. Downers Grove, IL: InterVarsity, 1970.

Sheldrake, Philip. *Spirituality and Theology: Christian Living and the Doctrine of God*. Maryknoll, NY: Orbis, 1998.

Smedes, Lewis B. *Union with Christ: A Biblical View of the New Life in Jesus Christ*. Grand Rapids: Eerdmans, 1983.

Smith, James K. A. *Who's Afraid of Postmodernism?: Taking Derrida, Lyotard, and Foucault to Church*. Grand Rapids: Baker Academic, 2006.

Smith, Christian, and Patricia Snell. *Souls in Transition: The Religious and Spiritual Lives of Emerging Adults*. New York: Oxford University Press, 2009.

Spidlik, Tomas. *The Spirituality of the Christian East: A Systematic Handbook*. Kalamazoo, MA: Cistercian, 1986.

Schaff, Philip, and Henry Wace, eds.. *Ante-Nicene Fathers*. Vol. 1, *Apostolic Fathers, Justin Martyr, Irenaeus*. Peabody, MA: Hendrickson, 1999.

―――, eds. *Nicene and Post-Nicene Fathers*. 2nd series. Vol. 4, *Athanasius, Select Works and Letters*. Peabody, MA: Hendrickson, 1999.

Stăniloae, Dumitru. *Orthodox Dogmatic Theology*. Brookline, MA: Holy Cross Orthodox Seminary Press, 2000.

―――. *Orthodox Spirituality: A Practical Guide for the Faithful and a Definitive Manual for the Scholar*. South Canaan, PA: St. Tikhon's Seminary Press, 2002.

Stone, Allucquere R. *The War of Desire and Technology at the Close of the Mechanical Age*. Cambridge: MIT Press, 1996.

Stone, Sandy. "Transgender." Would You Like Theory with That? http://www.sandystone.com/trans.shtml.

Sweet, Leonard I. *Post-Modern Pilgrims: First Century Passion For the 21st Century World*. Nashville: Broadman & Holman, 2000.

Tarnas, Richard. *The Passion of the Western Mind*. New York: Ballantine, 1991.

Tickle, Phyllis. *Emergence Christianity: What It Is, Where It Is Going, and Why It Matters*. Grand Rapids: Baker, 2012.

―――. *The Great Emergence: How Christianity Is Changing and Why*. Grand Rapids: Baker, 2008.

Tomlinson, Dave. *The Post Evangelical*. El Cajon, CA: Emergent YS/Zondervan, 2003.

Tucker, Kenneth H., Jr. "Spiritualties of Life: New Age Romanticism and Consumptive Capitalism." *American Journal of Sociology* 115 (2009) 920–22.

Veith, Gene Edward. *Postmodern Times: A Christian Guide to Contemporary Thought and Culture*. Wheaton, IL: Crossway, 1994.

Vlachos, Hierotheos. *Orthodox Psychotherapy: The Science of the Fathers*. Translated by Esther Williams. Levadia, Greece: Birth of the Theotokos Monastery, 1994.

Voegelin, Eric. *Science, Politics, and Gnosticism: Two Essays*. Washington, DC: Regnery, 1997.

Ware, Timothy. *The Orthodox Church*. London: Penguin, 1963.

―――. *The Orthodox Way*. Crestwood, NY: St. Vladimir's Seminary Press, 1979.

Warren, Rick. "Rick Warren on Peter Drucker and the Character of Great Leaders." http://www.youtube/?q=Rick+Warren +on+Peter+Drucker.

Watts, Alan. *The Book: On the Taboo against Knowing Who You Are*. New York: Vintage, 1989.

Weaver, Richard M. *Ideas Have Consequences*. Chicago: University of Chicago, 1948.

Webber, Robert. *Ancient-Future Faith: Rethinking Evangelicalism for a Postmodern World.* Grand Rapids: Baker, 1999.

Weil, Andrew. *The Natural Mind: A New Way of Looking at Drugs and the Higher Consciousness.* Boston: Houghton Mifflin, 1972.

Wells, David F. *No Place for Truth: Or Whatever Happened to Evangelical Theology?* Grand Rapids: Leicester, 1993.

Wheatley, Margaret J. *Leadership and the New Science: Discovering Order in a Chaotic World.* San Francisco: Berrett-Koehler, 2006.

White, Heath. *Postmodernism 101: A First Course for the Curious Christian.* Grand Rapids: Brazos, 2006.

White, James Emery. *What Is Truth?: A Comparative Study of the Positions of Cornelius Van Til, Francis Schaeffer, Carl F. H. Henry, Donald Bloesch, Millard Erickson.* Eugene, OR: Wipf and Stock, 2006.

"Why Christian Colleges Are Booming." *Christianity Today*, April 26, 1999. http://www.christianitytoday.com/ct/1999/april26/9t5026.html.

Wicker, Christine. *The Fall of the Evangelical Nation: The Surprising Crisis Inside the Church.* New York: HarperOne, 2008.

Willard, Dallas, and Jan Johnson. *Hearing God: Developing a Conversational Relationship with God.* Updated and expanded ed. Downers Grove, IL: Formatio, 2012.

Zizioulas, John D. *Being as Communion: Studies in Personhood and the Church.* Crestwood, NY: St. Vladimir's Seminary Press, 1985.

Zukav, Gary. *The Dancing Wu Li Masters: An Overview of the New Physics.* New York: Morrow, 1979.

Subject Index

Subject Index

Maranatha, 41
Maronite Catholicism, xv
Middle Ages, x
Millennials, 85, 88, 125
Modernity, 12–13, 29–30, 65, 126
Monasticism, 120
Mt. Athos, 123
Mysterium Tremendum, 99
Mystery, 8, 130
Mysticism, 16, 129–130
Mystics, 5

New Age, 81, 84
New Finnish School, 128
New Man, 128
Newtonian Physics, 78
Nominalism, 26
Nones, 51–52, 54, 88

Oikonomia, 115
Original Sin, 16
Orthodoxy, 40–41, 118

Pentecostals, 101
Pew, 51
Physicists, 77
Plan of Salvation, 11, 96–97, 101, 104
Platonism, 14
Postmodern, 93
Postmodernism, 65
Postmodernity, 63, 85
Premodern, 14, 112
Premodernity, 15–16, 67
Principica Mathmatica, 29
Protestant, 23
Protestant Christianity, ix,
Protestant Reformation, 119
Ptolemaic, 27–28

Puritan, 34

Quantum physics, 72, 78

Rationalism, 24, 35, 48
Reenchantment, 83
Reformation, 18, 22, 24, 127
Reformers, 127
Religious Roundtable, 44
Religious Right, 49
Renaissance, x, 17–18, 24, 30
Roman Catholic Church, 1, 21
Roman Catholicism, xv,

Saddleback Church, 42
Salvation, 127–128
Sanctification, 127
Scholasticism, 26
Sola Fide, 22
Sola Scriptura, 22–23, 111, 117–118
Soteriology, 10, 109

Taboric Light, 123–124
Telos, 15, 104, 106, 115
Theosis, xviii, 99–100, 102, 104–106,
    108–109, 111–112, 119–120, 127
Tradition, 117–118
Trinity Magazine, 41

Union (with God), 5, 7, 102, 106, 110,
    117, 126

Vatican II, 2
Vineyard Movement, 42

Youth for Christ, 39

Zeitgeist, 69, 72
Zen, 69

Author Index